God is Always Bigger

God is Always Bigger

Reflections by a Hopeful Critic

JOHN P. BOWEN

foreword by Susan J. A. Bell

WIPF & STOCK · Eugene, Oregon

GOD IS ALWAYS BIGGER
Reflections by a Hopeful Critic

Copyright © 2021 John P. Bowen. All rights reserved. Except for brief quotations in critical publications or reviews, no part of this book may be reproduced in any manner without prior written permission from the publisher. Write: Permissions, Wipf and Stock Publishers, 199 W. 8th Ave., Suite 3, Eugene, OR 97401.

Unless otherwise indicated, all Scripture quotations are taken from the New Revised Standard Version Bible: Anglicized Edition, copyright © 1989, 1995 National Council of the Churches of Christ in the United States of America. Used by permission. All rights reserved worldwide.

Wipf & Stock
An Imprint of Wipf and Stock Publishers
199 W. 8th Ave., Suite 3
Eugene, OR 97401

www.wipfandstock.com

PAPERBACK ISBN: 978-1-7252-8860-7
HARDCOVER ISBN: 978-1-7252-8859-1
EBOOK ISBN: 978-1-7252-8861-4

12/31/20

To the graduates of Wycliffe College,
with my heartfelt love and respect—
unsung heroes of the church

O Christ my Lord, again and again I have said with Mary Magdalene,

"They have taken away my Lord and I know not where they have laid him."

I have been desolate and alone. And thou hast found me again,

and I know that what has died is not thou, my Lord,

but only my idea of thee, the image which I have made

to preserve what I have found, and to be my security.

I shall make another image, O Lord, better than the last.

That too must go, and all successive images,

until I come to the blessed vision of thyself,

O Christ, my Lord.

GEORGE APPLETON, *THE OXFORD BOOK OF PRAYER*, #498

Contents

Illustrations | ix
Foreword by Susan J. A. Bell | xi
Introduction | 1

A. SIGNATURE SERMONS | 5

1. The School of Jesus (Matthew 11:28–30) | 7
2. Who Washes Whose Feet? (John 13:1–17) | 13
3. The Spiritual Quality of Craziness (Matthew 25:14–31) | 19
4. The Snag with Community (2 Corinthians 3:18) | 25
5. Redeeming the Idols (Jeremiah 2:12–14) | 30
6. God is Always Bigger | 35

B. FACETS OF SPIRITUALITY | 41

7. Five Spiritualities in the Body of Christ | 43
8. Ignatius for Non-Catholics? | 52
9. In Praise of Pietism | 57
10. "What are You Giving Up for Lent?": A Meditation on Mortification | 60
11. Getting Good and Angry | 64

C. WORLDLY WISDOM | 69

12. Vacuum Cleaner Church | 71
13. Serving God on the Inside and on the Outside | 75
14. The Vocation of a Garbage Collector | 80
15. Discipleship on the Front Lines | 85

D. SERMONS FOR SPECIAL OCCASIONS | 93

16 A Homily for the Wedding of Anna and Benjamin (John 2:1–12) | 95
17 My Mother's Funeral | 100
18 The Funeral of My Canadian Mother (Romans 8:18–39) | 103
19 The Day the Archbishop Came to Chapel (John 17:1–11) | 107
20 An Evangelist among the Scientists: Your Jesus is Too Small (Colossians 1:15–20) | 110
21 A Camp Reunion: The Leaders in Training from 1986 | 115
22 Having the Last Word: Faith for the Future (Hebrews 11:8–12, 17–19) | 119

E. SPEAKING FOR MYSELF | 125

23 Strong and Weak by Andy Crouch: A Personal Case Study | 127
24 Is "Anglican Evangelical" an Oxymoron? | 132
25 Spirituality in My Sixties | 136
26 The Christmas Gift I Never Asked for or Expected | 144
27 How (Not) to Ask for Money: True Confessions of a Fundraiser | 147

F. REDEEMING DOCTRINE | 151

28 Why Arius was Wrong | 153
29 Impossible Things before Breakfast 1 | 156
30 Impossible Things before Breakfast 2: He Descended into Hell | 162
31 Impossible Things before Breakfast 3: Six Ways to Believe in the Resurrection (John 20:24–29) | 166
32 What on Earth is Justification? | 171
33 What's Wrong with Amazing Grace? | 174

G. GOOD NEWS ABOUT EVANGELISM | 181

34 Humanizing Evangelism (John 1:35–51) | 183
35 Four Doors into Faith | 191
36 Are Evangelists Born or Made? | 195
37 How Does Evangelism Happen? A Study in Teamwork | 199
38 The Way I See it: Believing is Seeing | 202
39 Will They Come Back Next Week? The Challenge of Preaching at Christmas | 207
40 O Come, O Come, Emmanuel: Liturgy and Evangelism | 211

Bibliography | 215

Illustrations

A spiritual hierarchy 1 | 86
A spiritual hierarchy 2 | 86
The swoop of grace | 165
Two women | 204

Foreword

"Sermons are dangerous things. None goes out of church as he came in but either better or worse."[1]

These words speak a hopeful truth: whether or not a preacher be able, the hearer's heart is undoubtedly moved one way or another.

Luckily, we are in safe hands here with John Bowen's collected sermons and articles—and yet there is still a risk. The danger in *this* instance is that, to quote another famous churchman, our hearts will be "strangely warmed"[2] by the witness and experience of this very able preacher, and that, after reading, we will be changed, our faith deepened, and our hearts tuned to Christ's.

The purpose of a sermon is to interpret the good news; to help us read our lives through the Scriptures in order to help the hearer live faithfully; and to prepare us to be part of the transformation of the whole creation begun in Jesus Christ.

John's sermons and articles attempt all that, and are special in a few particulars. First, they were offered in varied circumstances and to much more diverse constituencies than preachers usually have access to. This has formed their substance in ways that are significant. They are invitational, and they are carefully constructed works of evangelistic and interpretive substance.

His long experience of introducing people to Jesus through InterVarsity Christian Fellowship is foundational to his style. He speaks as a loving interpreter, and his words act as gentle hands that convey the hearer

1. Herbert, *Country Parson*, 62.
2. Southey, *Life of John Wesley*, 119.

into God's waiting embrace. John doesn't pull any punches, however. The many experiences of life are dealt with in these pages: learning to live our Christian vocation every day without fanfare but with integrity, processing grief, praying through spiritual dryness, the seeming illogicality and impossibility of faith, but also the joy and exhilaration of belief in God and the unexpected journey it takes us on—all of these things are refracted through John's own experience as a disciple of Jesus.

The only thing better than reading John's words is to have the pleasure of hearing him deliver them in person. I have been fortunate on several occasions to witness John's gentle, but firm and winsome, manner—and this shines through in this homiletical collection.

A note to the reader: the sermon for which this book is named, "God is Always Bigger," is a good place to start. It is the foundation for so much of what this book promises.

To encounter all of these words is to receive a blessing. I commend them to your attention and the result of the reading to our Lord.

+SUSAN
The Right Reverend Susan J. A. Bell
Bishop of Niagara

Introduction

YOU MIGHT THINK THAT two people, especially two British people married for half a century, could agree on a simple thing like making tea. But no.

My approach is, well, rational. Two teabags are required to make a full pot and provide four cups of tea, thus one bag for half a pot and two cups. I will therefore boil enough water for either half a pot or a full pot, as needed. Waste not, want not. I assume you agree.

Deborah's approach, however, is much more—hmm, what's the kindest word?—wasteful. (Others might call it generous, I realize.) Her default is to make a full pot, on the off-chance that one of us might want a second cup. Well, sometimes we do, and sometimes we don't. And if neither of us has a second cup, then a whole half-pot and a whole teabag goes to waste. You see the problem? My preference—did I mention it is rational?—is to make a second half-pot only when someone asks for a second cup and not before, so that it's fresh.

If you are into personality types, none of this will surprise you, especially if you know Deborah and myself. If you hate personality types, I won't irritate you with that kind of explanation. You may be like my friend who said, "My four letters are B-E-T-H." Of course, for some of us, that tells us a lot about her personality type—"Just what I would expect someone of your type to say"—but it's probably just as well not to tell her that.

All this is a long way around to say that this book is a typical product of someone of my type. Since childhood, I have been a collector—coins, stamps, Scout badges, train numbers, matchbox labels (you can look it up), and even the numbers on car number plates (not the plates, just the numbers). In adulthood, I like to think this instinct has found more sophisticated expression—theology books (preferably secondhand, since that saves money), classical CDs, photographs, etymologies. For a time, I also collected old ladies, but now they are increasingly my age, so I have stopped.

Recently, we have had fun collecting androgynous first names—think Ashley, Mackenzie, Jordan, and Morgan, for a start. (No, do not send me your favorite examples, thank you. And no links to websites where someone has already done the work for you, either. That's cheating.) Of course, I am aware that the collection of cardboard boxes in the basement may not appear as sophisticated as all that, but you never know when they will come in handy.

Among the things I have collected for many years are sermon notes going back over forty years. The early ones are meticulously handwritten on loose-leaf paper which I used to carry in a pocket-sized Filofax binder (something else to look up); the more recent ones are written with two fingers on my laptop, of course.

So what is someone of this collector type (I will refrain from giving it a number or a four-letter designation) to do? The way for someone like me to grow spiritually is simple: to give away the stuff we collect. I recently gave away three-quarters of the boxes in the basement to a young family who were moving house, and it felt good.

That's why a lot of people of like me become teachers. Teaching is the perfect environment in which to give away all the stuff we have been accumulating in our heads, not to mention our libraries and our laptops. In fact, I believe it is the God-given way to turn what can degenerate into sheer miserliness into something life-giving, both for the giver and (hopefully) for the recipients.

WHY THIS BOOK?

That desire to give is, I suppose, behind this book. As my friend Michael Pountney has written, others "have worked and produced books like this and often talked of leaving a legacy." But I agree with his comment, "The whole idea of a legacy is far too overblown for me—I'm not into anything as grandiose as that. . . . I am not a legacy-leaving kind of man."[1]

I have struggled with whether doing a book like this is self-indulgent, even narcissistic. Am I doing it simply because I like the sound of my own voice? Publishers always want to know, "What is going to make someone want to buy this book?" It's a fair question. And I am embarrassed by the obvious answer: in this case, the only people likely to buy it are people who

---

1. Pountney, *Michael's Page*, x.

know me, and are interested in what I might have to say. But, for all I know, nobody was paying attention when these pieces were written or spoken in the first place!

There's a memory I have of a visit to Kenya in the early 2000s which helps me resolve this. We arrived in what my priest friend, Kistos, called "a Christian village." "Now," he said, "I'm going to gather all the people under this tree, and then I want you to teach us something from the Bible." I objected as politely as I could. How could I, a white European male, possibly stand under a mango tree, instructing a group of Africans sitting on the ground, from the Bible? The optics were terrible, and I would feel so incredibly uncomfortable.

I don't recall Kistos's exact words, but I am sure it was more polite than I remember: "I thought you said you had come here to serve us in whatever way we need? Well, right now, we need you to share what God has given you with these people, so please do what I am asking you!" In other words, this is your job—you're supposed to be a teacher—so please get on and do it. Your fine feelings are neither here nor there. Get over yourself. So I did, of course. I just didn't let anybody take a photograph.

A

Signature Sermons

I SUSPECT ALL PREACHERS have themes, or passages of Scripture, we love to preach on, and return to whenever we can get away with it. Of course, there are other themes and Scriptures most preachers try to avoid until they are pressed upon us for one reason or another—who finds it easy to preach on Abraham's call to sacrifice Isaac?—and I've had my share of those too.

These six sermons represent some of the texts and themes I have been most drawn to over the years. (There are a few others, and they appear elsewhere in this book—chapters 20 and 25, in particular.) I resist calling them my "favorite" sermons, because they're not all comfortable, at least for me, but they have been formative for me, and so it seemed important to include them at the start of this book.

1

The School of Jesus

Matthew 11:28–30

Sometime in the 1980s, I met Bob Brow. He had been a missionary in India, but when I knew him he was Rector of St. James's Anglican Church in Kingston, Ontario, on the edge of the prestigious Queen's University campus. He had recently written a book, controversial at the time, called Go, Make Learners. In this, he explained the image I explore here, that one fruitful way to think of the church is as the school of Jesus. Like any good metaphor, I found it shed light on a number of previously unrelated things.

The idea has stuck with me for many years, and has reappeared in many forms and contexts. Someone said, "What the church needs is not better arguments but better metaphors." I think that's right. Metaphors help us see familiar things in a fresh light, and in my experience this image is one that readily connects with people both inside and outside the church. It is not the only metaphor for the church, of course, but it is often a helpful starting point. This version was preached at St. George's Anglican Church in St. Catharines (and yes, that is the correct punctuation!), Ontario, in June, 2016.

> "Come to me, all you that are weary
> and are carrying heavy burdens,
> and I will give you rest.
> Take my yoke upon you, and learn from me;
> for I am gentle and humble in heart,

> and you will find rest for your souls.
> For my yoke is easy, and my burden is light."
> (Matt 11:28–30)

One of the things we have been learning in recent years is to call people what they want to be called. So, we no longer talk about Eskimos, we talk about the Inuit. We don't talk about Indians any more, but about First Nations—although one Cree friend said, "Hey, we're Indians. We call ourselves Indians. You can call us Indians." But I don't, and I won't. We have more or less learned to speak of Asians, not Orientals, and so on.

Personally, I am waiting for this principle to be applied to my own nationality, the Welsh. You probably don't know what the word "Welsh" means, so let me tell you. It is an Old English word meaning "foreigner." The Welsh word for a Welsh person is *Cymro* (male) or *Cymraes* (female). But I'm not holding my breath.

Another name that should maybe be changed is the name Christian. After all, it isn't a term Christians chose for themselves. It occurs only three times in the New Testament, and on two of those occasions it is in the mouth of someone not themselves Christian.

So what did the first Christians call themselves? There are various words, but the most common one is the word "disciple." They were disciples of Jesus. Now, of course, disciple is a fairly unusual word these days, and in church circles it means almost exclusively the twelve apostles. But it's not really a religious word at all. It's simply the word for a student, which means those first disciples must have thought of the church as (among other things) a school.

Of course, that raises some interesting questions: What is this school for? What do you learn there? Where does it take place, and how? And is it true that the graduate courses are out of this world?

The easiest one is: Who is the teacher? The answer (of course) is Jesus. In the heart of today's reading is an invitation from him: "Learn from me." He is calling people, not to be religious, not even to be nice people, but to be his disciples, his students.

Then I think we want to ask: What is this school about? Jesus announced good news—he called it the good news of God's kingdom—that through him, his life, death, and resurrection, God is at work to put to rights everything that is wrong in the world. And students of Jesus are those who have accepted his invitation, and are learning from him how to play their part in that work.

Another way of putting this idea is to say that the school of Jesus is a school for life. In the 1940s, Dorothy Sayers wrote a play cycle on the life of Christ called *The Man Born to be King* for the BBC in Britain. In one episode, she puts into the mouth of Mary Magdalene a speech in which she explains to Jesus why she wanted to become a disciple:

> "Did you know? My friends and I came there that day to mock you. We thought you would be sour and grim, hating all beauty and treating life as an enemy. But when I saw you, I was amazed. You were the only person there who was really alive. The rest of us were going about half-dead—making the gestures of life, pretending to be real people. The life was not with us but with you—intense and shining, like the strong sun when it rises and turns the flames of our candles to pale smoke. And I wept and was ashamed, seeing myself such a thing of trash and tawdry. But when you spoke to me, I felt the flame of the sun in my heart. I came alive for the first time. And I love life all the more since I have learnt its meaning."[1]

Jesus lives a fully human life, in complete harmony with God. As a result, he demonstrates a beauty and authenticity that can be deeply compelling to those who are seeking it. Mary thought she knew what life was all about—until she met Jesus and joined the company of those who were learning the kind of life he lived.

Where do classes happen? Well, unlike most students' experience, the heart of Jesus' school is not in a classroom, listening to lectures. In fact, "student" may not be the best translation of the word "disciple"; I am beginning to think "apprentice" would be a more accurate term.

My friend Ken is an electrician. When I was preaching on this topic at my own church once, I invited Ken to come up and tell us how he became an electrician. The answer was simple: "On Mondays, we went to electrician school, and heard lectures about being an electrician. Then from Tuesday to Friday we were out on the job with a master electrician, learning little by little to do what they did." Isn't that how the disciples of Jesus learned? Yes, there were some lectures—think the Sermon on the Mount—but most of the time they were on the road with Jesus, watching him preach and heal, welcome the outcasts, and confront religious hypocrisy. In fact, maybe we need to go beyond saying Jesus is running a school, and say instead that he is running a trade school.

Because this is what it is like, this school of Jesus operates anywhere and anytime, 24/7. Anything that comes our way in the course of a day can be an opportunity to learn. It may be an annoying person, a moral dilemma, a new responsibility, someone asking for our help, an opportunity

---

1. Sayers, *Man Born to be King*, 186–87.

to forgive, an invitation to be generous . . . Everything that happens is raw material for the teacher to use to shape us for the kingdom, and through us to shape the world.

Are the standards high? Well, you know the answer already: yes. Basically, our teacher is training us to be like him—there could be no higher standard!—and that will take all we have and all we are. The process will change us in uncomfortable ways.

Fortunately, the teacher says, "I am humble and gentle"—unlike some teachers we may have known. Jesus doesn't use sarcasm or intimidation. He understands our limitations and our sinfulness. He is a patient teacher.

He also says, "Take my yoke upon you." Before we came to Canada, I had never seen an ox with a yoke. I think I assumed that meant I was the ox, and that Jesus laid his yoke across my neck and walked behind, guiding the plow. Shortly after we came to Toronto, however, we went to an old farm where everything was as it had been in the nineteenth century.

And there we saw something that completely changed my understanding of Jesus' words. We saw a plow being pulled by two oxen, wearing a double yoke. Our guide explained that the double yoke was often used to connect an older, more experienced ox to a young ox so that, as they plowed together, the older one would teach the younger one how to do it.

A light went on. I'm sure you saw it before I did. That's what Jesus means. He already knows how to wear the yoke of being human, and pulling the plow of working in God's world. And his invitation to us is to share his yoke as the junior partner, and learn from him how to live a kingdom life.

There is one more encouragement here. I'm not a Greek scholar, but I am told the word translated here as "easy" in the phrase "my yoke is easy" is better translated, "well-fitting." Apparently, in Jesus' day, if you had a new ox, you didn't just buy an off-the-shelf, one-size-fits-all yoke from the local farm equipment store. Instead, you would take your ox to the carpenter's shop, and he would shape a yoke to fit the shoulders of your new ox and no other. It was truly a "well-fitting" yoke.

I don't know about you, but I find that so encouraging. In the trade school of Jesus, the curriculum is individually shaped to every single apprentice. What Jesus is teaching me may well be different from what Jesus is teaching you. What Jesus is teaching my home church may well be different from what Jesus is teaching this congregation. That is for us to discern.

One more thing: How do you join the school? On the day when Jesus said these things, he began by saying, "Come to me." It was a very practical thing. My guess is that when he had finished speaking, and people were packing up and heading for home, there were some who didn't leave but went in the opposite direction. Perhaps they excused themselves from their family group, and just said, "I'll see you later. There's something I have to do."

I imagine them coming up to Jesus, maybe a bit embarrassed, slightly hesitant—what on earth were they getting into?—and saying to him, "Jesus, you know what you were saying about learning from you, and taking your yoke, and all that? Um, do you think I could be your apprentice and begin hanging out with you?" And I imagine Jesus smiling a broad smile and saying, "That's great. You are very welcome. We're just going for supper. Come and meet the others, and we'll talk. What's your name?"

How do you join the school? Basically, by asking. I don't know who you are this morning. But my guess is that you are hearing this and responding in a number of different ways.

- You may be visiting today, and not a regular churchgoer. Maybe this idea of the church as the trade school of Jesus intrigues you. There is a traditional way in which Christians register for the school of Jesus, and that's through baptism. If you have never been baptized, but you are thinking about what it would mean to become a student of Jesus, talk to the minister about baptism.

- Some here today may be students already. You know you are in the school and you are trying to learn from Jesus every day, however stumblingly. (Frankly, I don't think there is any other way.) I hope these words this morning encourage you to keep following and to keep learning.

- But maybe you are thinking, "Hmm, I think I've been a part-time student up to now, and it's not working very well. Maybe it's time I bit the bullet and went full-time. I would get so much more out of it. It's difficult living in two worlds as I am doing right now." OK, tell Jesus that.

- It's also possible you are saying to yourself, "You know, I used to be a keen student, but recently I've played hooky rather a lot. So I've missed a lot of classes and I'm way behind on my assignments." If that's you, believe me, it is never too late to start over. Jesus can sort out whatever mess you may have got yourself into, and you can restart classes even today.

- Finally, you may even have been involved in church for a long time, but you knew you were missing something somewhere, and this is making a lot of sense. You want to respond.

Although Jesus is not here in the flesh, he is just as much here today as he was on the day when he first said these words. And he says them afresh today to us:

"Come to me, all you that are weary and are carrying heavy burdens, and I will give you rest. Take my yoke upon you, and learn from me; for I am gentle and humble in heart, and you will find rest for your souls. For my yoke is easy, and my burden is light."

To all of us, Jesus says, "Come." Let us pray.

> Lord Jesus.
> Thank you for living a fully human life in our world.
> Thank you too for your invitation
> to become your apprentices and learn from you.
> We are grateful for your words that
> you are a gentle and humble teacher.
> Lord, we are all different,
> but we are grateful that you know
> what lessons each of us needs to learn.
> Whoever we are, help us say yes to you this morning.
> And as we come to you, please come to us.
> Receive us, teach us, make us your apprentices,
> shape us into the people you know we can become.
> Amen.

2

Who Washes Whose Feet?

John 13:1–17

A NUMBER OF THE sermons in this book were originally preached at my home church, St. John the Evangelist Anglican Church, affectionately known as the Rock on Locke (that is, Locke Street), in Hamilton, Ontario. We moved here in 1996, and settled at St. John's in 1997. Over that time, this church has become home and family to us. We love this community and have been wonderfully cared for by them.

The nature of my work has for years meant that I am frequently a guest preacher in churches where I don't know anyone apart from the minister, and where I get to choose my own topic. There is a freedom about this, colloquially known as "preach and run."

Consequently, it is both a treat and a challenge to preach in my own community. A treat, because I know most of the people and something of their situation, and they know me. And a challenge . . . well, for exactly the same reasons. Preaching on my home turf also means in general that I preach on whatever the text for the day is, and that forces me out of my comfort zone, which is a good discipline.

This sermon is from Lent 2008, and is one in a series called, "What's so Amazing about Grace?" I chose the approach I did because we are a very activist community—an Energizer Bunny among churches—which is good, of course, but can become unbalanced.

> During supper Jesus, knowing that the Father had given all things into his hands, and that he had come from God and was going to God, got up from the table, took off his outer robe, and tied a towel around himself. Then he poured water into a basin and began to wash the disciples' feet and to wipe them with the towel that was tied around him. He came to Simon Peter, who said to him, 'Lord, are you going to wash my feet?' Jesus answered, 'You do not know now what I am doing, but later you will understand.' Peter said to him, 'You will never wash my feet.' Jesus answered, 'Unless I wash you, you have no share with me.' Simon Peter said to him, 'Lord, not my feet only but also my hands and my head!' Jesus said to him, 'One who has bathed does not need to wash, except for the feet, but is entirely clean.'
> ... After he had washed their feet, had put on his robe, and had returned to the table, he said to them, 'Do you know what I have done to you? You call me Teacher and Lord—and you are right, for that is what I am. So if I, your Lord and Teacher, have washed your feet, you also ought to wash one another's feet. For I have set you an example, that you also should do as I have done to you. Very truly, I tell you, servants are not greater than their master, nor are messengers greater than the one who sent them. If you know these things, you are blessed if you do them (John 13:3–10a, 12–17).

The biographies of Jesus we call the Gospels are different from other biographies in a number of ways. One is that they spend such a long time talking about the death of Jesus and what happened afterwards. Roughly 20 percent of the Gospels is spent talking about the final week of Jesus' life—which tells you something of how important they thought it was.

But this feature creates a problem for those whose job is to try to teach and preach the Christian faith—because traditionally the stories of Jesus' death are remembered in just one particular week of the year—the week leading up to Easter. That means one-fifth of the stories about Jesus have to be taught in about one-fiftieth of the year!

All this is a long way round to tell you I want to talk this morning about a story that really belongs three weeks from now, in Easter Week—to be precise, on Maundy Thursday, the day before Good Friday, and I want to do it now so that we have a bit more leisure to think about it.

It's the story of Jesus washing the disciples' feet. Here's my question for you: What exactly is the point of this story? I used to think it was the command that we should wash one another's feet—and maybe you do too. Now I'm not so sure.

Sometimes in churches on Maundy Thursday, there are foot-washing ceremonies. After all, it's a pretty clear command: "If I have washed your feet, you also ought to wash one another's feet" (14). But if you have ever been to one, your reaction may have been the same as mine. Either I find I have a pressing engagement elsewhere at the same time, or (if I really can't get out of it) at least to make sure I have washed my feet and put on clean socks before I go. For us, the idea of having someone wash our feet is just, well, weird.

Not so in Jesus' time. Sandals were normal, there were no paved roads, and the weather was generally hot and dry. At the end of a journey, your feet would be tired, dusty, and even blistered. So you would arrive at your friend's house and sit down, and a servant would take a basin and towel, remove your sandals, and wash your feet. In that culture, this was perfectly normal. You wouldn't think twice about it.

So let me ask you: How do you imagine people felt when someone washed their feet? Normally, I think, you would feel cared for, welcomed, refreshed, and ready for anything.

But on this occasion, the one who did the foot-washing was Jesus, their "lord and teacher." How did they feel now? I imagine the effect would be almost precisely the opposite. It must have made them deeply uncomfortable, paralyzed with embarrassment, and longing to get away. Peter simply articulates what they were all feeling but didn't know how to put into words: "Lord, this just isn't right!" Most times when they had had their feet washed it was totally unmemorable. Not so this one. The memory of this occasion would burn in them for the rest of their lives.

This story and the command that follows—"I have set you an example, that you also should do as I have done to you"—have inspired Christians for centuries. Let me give you just one example. My friend Joe gave up a job which paid $60,000 in Calgary, Alberta, in order to start a new church in Sarnia, Ontario. That meant his income dropped to $12,000—the size of his expense account in his old job. What is it that motivates people to do such crazy things? It's simple: Jesus was Joe's "lord and teacher," and this was a way Jesus asked Joe to wash other people's feet.

People here at St. John's wash other people's feet in different ways. We work hard. We send teams to work in a hospital in Haiti. We collect food for St. Matthew's House. We serve meals to the homeless at Out of the Cold. We teach Sunday school and run Bible studies, and work on committees and sing in the choir. We bake casseroles—a lot of casseroles—for sick neighbors. We give sacrificially to these things of our time, talent, and treasure. Why? You don't have to look very far to know that we too are trying to obey our Savior's example: "you also should do as I have done to you."

Now here's a health warning. It's very easy to use this story as a stick to beat ourselves up: Try harder, give more, work longer hours, increase your tithe, volunteer for this, that, and the other. Come on, folks: there are lots more dusty, blistered feet out there, and it is your responsibility as good Christians to get out there and wash them. That's what Jesus wants. Follow his example! Right? Well, yes. But also no. You may ask, "What do you mean, no? Surely those are all good things? Aren't those at the heart of our faith?" But, folks, that's not the gospel.

In this series, we're thinking about amazing grace. If this story only means we should try harder, then it's not grace: it's just another law, it's a burden religion lays on us. But I actually think this story is about grace. We often miss the point of the story. And what is that? It's simple, really. Are you ready? We need to let Jesus wash our feet. "I have set you an example, that you also should do as I have done to you."

Think of it this way. If you could ask the disciples ten years after this night what they remembered, what do you think it would be? "Ah yes, that's the night Jesus laid this huge burden on us to go and serve needy and hurting people everywhere." And they would sigh, and go get another basin and towel.

I highly doubt it. You ask them about that scene in the Upper Room, and they would give a quite different answer. Let's say it's Bartholomew. He would tell you about the actual supper, of course, and how Jesus blessed the bread and wine. He might remember (though he hardly noticed at the time) Judas slipping from the room. He would remember snippets of the teaching Jesus gave.

And then you would ask, "But I heard he also washed your feet. Is that right?" And there would be a silence, and he would look away, and you would realize with embarrassment that he had tears in his eyes. Finally, he would say, "It's true. It was wonderful . . . and terrible. It was so intimate, and so scary. I was very glad he was doing it, and utterly embarrassed. And I think it was then, at that moment, for the first time, I realized how much he loved me." Another long silence. "That changed my life, you know. And it still sustains me today, all these years afterwards."

In other words, I do not for one instant believe the first thing they would remember was Jesus' command to wash other people's feet; that came afterwards. "We love," says the apostle John, "because he first loved us" (1 John 4:19). Maybe he was remembering that night too. God's love is the cause of our loving; our love is merely the result. This is one of the things that is distinctive about Christianity. It never begins with what we do for God but with what God does for us. It's about God's love for us and our neighbor—and only then about our love for God and our neighbor. If we get these the wrong way around, it will damage our spiritual health, and maybe that of those whose feet we wash too.

We teach our children, "Jesus loves me, this I know," so we think it's kids' stuff—yet it's difficult to believe. "Jesus loves me." Do we actually know it?

I think this is one reason Peter resists. It's hard to let yourself be loved. We always want to be up and doing, to prove ourselves, to make ourselves worthy. We don't want to sit still and have our feet washed. That's just human nature. But Jesus is very clear: unless we let him love us, "you have no share with me" (8)—we're not doing his work, we're just an organization of religious do-gooders.

William Temple, once the Archbishop of Canterbury, reflected on this story:

> We are ready, perhaps, to be humble before God; but we do not want him to be humble in his dealings with us. . . . Every disciple and every company of disciples begin by wanting to give service. . . . But every disciple and every company of disciples need to learn that their first duty is to let Christ serve them. . . . We would gladly wash the feet of the divine lord; he insists on washing ours.[1]

May I ask: How do you experience the love of Jesus? How does Jesus wash your feet? How does he want to wash your feet? Do you give him opportunities to do so?

- One way is to simply find a quiet place, read this story, and imagine yourself at the table. You are one of the disciples—and Jesus comes to you and washes your feet. What does it feel like? Imagine his face. What does he say to you?
- Here's another way to think of it. Every time we confess our sins and receive forgiveness, that is Jesus washing our feet. (I believe this is the distinction Jesus is making between foot-washing and complete washing in verse 10.)
- The word for "washing" or "cleansing" occurs elsewhere in John's Gospel. That being so, it's interesting to put John 15:3 alongside this story—"you are already cleansed by the word that I have spoken to you." In Jesus' understanding, his words are apparently a cleansing agent. Any time we have a sense of God speaking to us, whether through the Bible, or a sermon, or a friend—whether it's affirmation or challenge—that's Jesus washing our feet.

---

1. Temple, *Readings in John's Gospel*, 209, 212, 214.

Those are just examples, and I suspect you can add to my list. Maybe some are very personal, a way of Jesus washing your feet that is especially meaningful to you. However it may happen, I believe Jesus is seeking to wash our feet every day. The trouble is, we often don't notice when these things are happening, or we take them for granted, or we don't realize this is what they are.

Once we've begun to glimpse that Jesus loves us, then—and only then—should we begin to think about the second half of that statement: "I have set you an example, that you also should do as I have done to you." That's because Jesus washing our feet makes us feel cared for, welcomed, refreshed, and ready for anything. And that "anything" includes washing the feet of others, and so passing on that love of Jesus.

3

The Spiritual Quality of Craziness

Matthew 25:14–31

I FIRST LEARNED THE approach I take here to the parable of the talents from an IVCF (InterVarsity Christian Fellowship) colleague in Kingston, Ontario, Doug Caldwell, in the 1980s. I don't know if Doug ever really knew what a box was, otherwise I would have said he thought outside the box. His read on this and other parables was both refreshing and challenging, especially for those brought up to think Christianity is safe and respectable. For me, and for countless students of Doug's, this—along with his study on the parable of the (so-called) prodigal son, and the parable of the unjust steward—was life-changing.

This particular version is a sermon preached at St. Bride's Anglican Church in Mississauga, Ontario, in February of 2010.

There is a quality I find strangely lacking in Christian disciples today. It's not faith, or love, or even joy. You probably won't guess, so I'll tell you. It is the ancient and honorable quality of craziness.

You may say, "I've never heard of that as a spiritual quality. Where on earth do you find it in Scripture?" And it's true. There is no "Blessed are the crazy ones . . ." among the Beatitudes. Craziness does not appear as a tenth fruit of the Spirit. Neither does Paul include it among the things Christians should ponder, alongside "whatever things are true, honorable, just and pure."

Yet it is there. And today's gospel reading, traditionally called the parable of the talents, is precisely about this art. Perhaps you have known this parable for many years. It is often preached as a parable about being reliable and responsible stewards of our talents. Well, I used to think that, but no longer. Let's come at this by asking some questions about the story:

WHAT DID SERVANTS 1 AND 2 DO RIGHT?

Immediately, the story causes raised eyebrows—or it should. These two servants made a pile of money. One made 1,000 percent, the other 500 percent, on their investments. Even if this took several years—and the story doesn't say—this is amazing.

How on earth did they do this? What was their secret? We know the secret in general: if you want to make big bucks, the best way to do it is through . . . risky investments. It just doesn't happen through steady, safe, responsible investment. No, with risky investments, you may get rich, but there again maybe you will lose everything. There's no way of knowing.

So what exactly is Jesus recommending here? Undoubtedly, there is an element of hyperbole here, but the hyperbole is there to startle us and make us think. Is Jesus telling us to be gamblers? Should church treasurers take the Sunday offering to the casino as soon as it opens on Monday, and see if they can improve the church's bank balance? That would be . . . crazy. Hmmm.

One thing we need to do with puzzling Scriptures is to see how they compare with other places in Scripture. So is there anything, any story, that might encourage us to think this is the correct understanding of the parable? I can think of a few.

Take Abraham, for instance. A respectable businessman, and very successful. I can imagine him being a respected member of the city council of Uz for some years, a member of the board of trade, and an elder in his church. His life direction has long been clear. He is stable, reliable, a pillar of the Uz community.

Then one day he announces to all his friends and associates, "Friends, I'm going away."

"Where are you going, Abram? Is this a winter vacation?"

"I'm not entirely sure where I am going, except that it's to another country."

"What? Which country?"

"I don't know yet."

"But how long will you be gone?"

"I have no idea, but I have a feeling I will never come back."

"Abram, why on earth are you behaving like this?"

"Easy, really: out in the desert, I heard God's voice calling me."

Abram resigns from all his civic and church responsibilities, closes his bank accounts, cuts up his credit cards, and just walks off, followed by all his household and his flocks. What's the kindest thing people might say about him? "He must be crazy."

There you go.

Then there was that teenager called David. No sitting in the basement playing video games for him. Instead, what does he do? He goes out to fight a giant, a giant that has a whole army scared and ready to turn tail and run.

King Saul realizes that to accept David's offer to fight Goliath means almost certain death for this unarmed kid. So he makes what seems a sensible move, offering David his armor, but David is clearly not impressed by such prudential common sense, and refuses it.

Instead, he takes five stones and his slingshot. Have you ever wondered why he took five? According to the story, it only took one stone to defeat the giant. Sometimes the most natural explanation is the right one. I believe he didn't know how many shots it would take, and five was probably the maximum he thought he could get in against the giant before the giant got him. He had calculated the risk.

You may say, "But he knew God would give him victory, right?" Well David certainly had faith he would win: "This very day the Lord will deliver you into my hand, and I will strike you down and cut off your head" (1 Sam 17:46). But, if you look closely, this is one of those occasions when God is horribly silent. David sounds confident enough, but there has been no guarantee from God that everything will turn out right. Wow. This kid must be . . . crazy.

There's that word again.

I call as my third witness Queen Esther. It is the fifth century BCE. Esther is Jewish, but married to King Ahasuerus of Persia. Due to the enmity of Haman, the king's adviser, there is a plot to exterminate all the Jews in the kingdom. Esther's uncle, Mordecai, encourages her to use her influence to change the king's mind. However, she can't just wander into the king's presence unannounced to plead her case. Indeed, if you just blithely walk in when you are not wanted, it can cost you your life. Esther knows the risk, but approaches the king anyway. Thanks be to God, he is in a good mood, and, as a result, the plot begins to unravel and the Jews are saved. But the turning point of the whole story is clearly Esther's willingness to take a risk for God's people—a touch of craziness, wouldn't you say?

In all three instances, people who take risks, who demonstrate a willingness to act a little crazy, find praise and affirmation in the pages of the Old Testament. They invested their talents in risky but high-yield investments, and they paid off.

WHAT DID SERVANT 3 DO WRONG?

To answer this question, I need to use some language that is not very nice to use in church. Are you ready? If you feel you need to block your ears, I will understand. Servant number three was . . . sensible, respectable, cautious, and responsible, and he certainly didn't take risks. There! What do you think? I hope you weren't too horrified. It's pretty bad, isn't it? But I always feel it's good to call things by their proper names.

I do realize that some of you may be shocked that I am shocked. But you know what? The master in the story was shocked too. What had the servant done wrong? He doesn't appear to have done anything. He actually says, "I went and hid your talent in the ground. Here you have what is yours" (25). He did nothing—but in this case nothing was precisely the wrong thing to have done.

The whole point was the servant was supposed to do something. The very least he could have done was "to have invested my money with the bankers," (27) where there would have been at least a minimal rate of interest. But he didn't even do that.

Why didn't he do anything? He himself says he was afraid (21). The risks were too scary. What if he lost everything? He believes the master is "a harsh man" (24). (Personally, I don't think he is, and certainly the other two servants don't seem to have thought so, but we'll let that go for now.) The master has a different interpretation: he calls the servant "wicked and lazy" (26).

Why lazy? When you think about it, the other two servants worked hard. They must have checked out possible investments and calculated the different degrees of risk. Maybe they talked to the captains of trading ships, and asked about their cargoes. Perhaps they haggled with the traders. I wouldn't be surprised if they'd lain awake nights, worrying about their investments. Likely they read *The Financial Times* over breakfast with their coffee every day, and anxiously scanned the stock market reports.

The third servant did none of these. What did he do while the master was away? Well, the talent was safe enough. He didn't need to worry or even think about it. He could do whatever he liked with his days. By the master's criteria, yes, he certainly was lazy. After all, he was meant to be a servant, not a man of leisure!

Is this a new idea? One thing that is always helpful is to look at the context of a story. Both Matthew and Luke tell this story, though in slightly different forms. In Mathew's Gospel, on either side of this parable are other stories about Jesus' return and coming judgment. You can see why this story fits right in. But in Luke's Gospel, the context is different. There, the parable follows immediately on the heels of the story of Zacchaeus (Luke 19:1–10).

Why does that matter? You may remember the story of Zacchaeus, the tax collector who overcharges people and gets rich on the proceeds. Then he meets Jesus and everything changes. The about-face is radical. Listen to his words: "Look, half of my possessions, Lord, I will give to the poor; and if I have defrauded anyone of anything, I will pay back four times as much" (Luke 19:8). If he had stolen $1,000, he would repay $4,000. Gasp!

You know, he didn't stop to think this out, did he? He didn't talk to his accountant or his bank manager. Of course, they might have tried to stop him. They might have asked, "Zacchaeus, are you sure this is wise? What happens to your budget, and your stewardship of resources, and your savings for retirement, not to mention the payments on your Ferrari, if you do this? On balance, Zacchaeus, we would advise you not to do it. It would be, well, crazy." But Zacchaeus's spontaneous generosity seems to have made Jesus happy. I suspect he smiled broadly.

Then, in Luke's Gospel, Jesus goes immediately on to tell the parable of the talents, as though it is a commentary on what just happened to Zacchaeus, as though he is challenging all who consider themselves servants of God to imitate Zacchaeus's example. And maybe he is.

ARE THERE CRAZY CHRISTIANS AROUND TODAY?

Well, I've met quite a few. I think of a number who have given up lucrative careers in North America to go and serve in the Global South as doctors or educators. I think of one young friend, who was a promising, up-and-coming lawyer, who gave it all up to be an Anglican priest. A church planter I know moved with his family into the second-poorest neighborhood in Canada in order to build community and start a church in an area where there was none. One couple retired from their work of managing a summer camp, and instead of settling down comfortably at the cottage, spent several years with an organization called Mercy Ships, sailing round the world, offering medical help, food, and Christian resources to some of the most neglected parts of the world. Some retirement!

Now it's worth adding that for these people, and for every disciple, risks like this don't come every day. Ninety-nine percent of days are ordinary, undramatic, and routine. I guess this was even true for Zacchaeus as he learned to follow Jesus in his everyday life. None of us could live the stress of constant craziness, and I don't think we are meant to.

But there are moments every so often that are turning points in our lives, moments when the challenges to risk come along. Some of them are big and obvious, like choosing between career paths, or where to live. And some choices are more mundane, such as how to spend our out-of-work time, or whether to risk a difficult conversation. In my own life, I have experienced both kinds of opportunities to risk, to act a little crazy.

Tony Campolo tells the story of a survey done of fifty people aged ninety-five. (It was a small sample.) They were asked the obvious question: If you could live your life over again, what would you do differently? Their answers fell into three categories: they would take more risks, they would spend more time in reflection, and they would try to do more that would live on after them.

All three are worth thinking about, of course, but the first is the one that interests me the most: they would have taken more risks. How sad, to get to the end of one's life, and think, "Why was I so cautious? What was I afraid of? What more might I have achieved if I had been less concerned about comfort and predictability?"

Risk-taking, at least at the hinge moments of our lives, should be a normal part of the life of discipleship. Is it crazy? Not really. If we really believe the world is in God's hands and the Spirit of Jesus is present in the world to restore God's kingdom, then risk makes perfect sense. Indeed, the true craziness is to think we can follow Jesus without risk!

When you think about it, being a risk-taker is consistent with our faith. After all, the God we believe in is one who took the ultimate risk of giving up the comfort of heaven to enter into our world, even though it meant he got himself killed. People said he was crazy too.

Finally, there is one phrase in this story that we haven't looked at yet, but that we dare not overlook: the words of the master to the first two servants, "Well done, good and faithful servant" (Matt 25:21, 23 KJV). Those are the words we most want to hear. Those are the words that make everything worthwhile.

4

The Snag with Community

2 Corinthians 3:18

I DID MY DOCTOR of Ministry from 1994 till 1999 at McMaster Divinity College in Hamilton. In my third year, I was invited to speak at the service which ended the start-of-year retreat. The theme of the retreat, including the plenary talks and the small group times, was "Christian Community," so that's what I preached on.

The text is one I remember coming across and being struck by when I was an undergraduate. It has worked away at me over the years and got into my theological bloodstream, so I was grateful to have a suitable opportunity to preach about it. The spin I put on it here, however, was a new idea and just appealed to my sense of humor.

I should add that sermons are shaped to some extent by the community in which they are spoken. So this one pays more attention to the details of one particular verse, including the Greek and the grammar, than I would normally do in an ordinary local congregation.

I think I'm going to change my religion.

I used to like the idea that I could be guided by a book that gave me a clear shape and direction for my life. Now I'm not so sure. I think I'm going to look for one where the sacred books just give advice in a take-it-or-leave-it kind of way.

I'll tell you why I'm changing my mind. There is a verse in the Bible—maybe my favorite verse—that I've just noticed something about. And maybe it isn't my favorite verse any more—2 Corinthians 3:18:

> All of us, with unveiled faces, seeing the glory of the Lord as though reflected in a mirror, are being transformed into the same image from one degree of glory to another; for this comes from the Lord, the Spirit.

I love the fact that at the center of that verse is that awesome word "transformed." It's difficult to translate it strongly enough. The Greek word is used on only two other occasions in the New Testament, at the transfiguration ("he was transfigured before them," Mark 9:2) and in Romans 12:2 ("be transformed by the renewing of your minds"). The Greek word is *metamorphoo*, which always reminds me of Kafka's short story, "Metamorphosis," where the hero wakes up one morning to find he has been metamorphosed—transfigured—into a giant bug. The word is that radical—although, as we shall see, the effects are not always that horrific!

Shocking though it may seem, Paul is saying that I am being metamorphosed into Christ's likeness. That's amazing, if difficult to believe or even understand. God is etching the beauty of Jesus into my sinful human nature. God is chipping away at everything that is twisted and ugly and destructive in me—some of which I recognize and some of which I don't—and nurturing qualities that are like Jesus instead.

But there's more. The Greek word here for "image" is the same as is used in the Greek Old Testament in Genesis 1:26–27 for the image of God in human beings. So the image which is being shaped in me is not only that of Jesus, but is also the image of God. Not surprising, of course, when you factor in that Jesus is "the image of the invisible God" (Col 1:15). What is happening to me is that I am being shaped, or reshaped, into the kind of human being God intended from the very beginning. I am, if you like, a new Adam.

This leaves us asking: How exactly does this happen? Paul's answer here is by "seeing the glory of the Lord." I am changed as I see the glory of the Lord. He seems to be saying that every believer has, in some sense, seen Jesus. Where have we seen Jesus? Unlike Paul, we do not generally see Jesus in person, face to face, but primarily in Scripture. Yes, we certainly see Jesus in communion, and in the faces of others, and in creation—but we know to look for Jesus in those places because Scripture has taught us to find him there.

So I am changed as I see Jesus. There is scientific evidence that couples grow to look alike the longer they are together. The person doing this research concluded that "people, often unconsciously, mimic the facial expressions of their spouses in a silent empathy and that, over the years, sharing the same expressions shapes the face similarly."[1] Is it too whimsical to suggest that as we spend time looking at Jesus, in Scripture and in the world—finding joy in the things that delight him, and feeling grief at the things which break his heart—the more we grow more like God? Paul seems to think not.

He uses the image of a mirror: Jesus shines on me, and I reflect his glory to the world. Not that that is a perfect metaphor. A mirror is not changed by the light shining on it—but I am.

Does all this sound outrageous? I hope so. It certainly does to me. But it gets worse. Paul tells me it is none other than the Holy Spirit of God who undertakes to do this for me: "the Lord, the Spirit."[2] The Baptist scholar Tom Smail wrote: "This is in the end the most profound thing that can be said of [the Spirit]—he changes us into the likeness of the Lord."[3] Which is particularly thought-provoking because it comes from such a notable charismatic leader. The humility and condescension of God to remake his spoiled creation: me. Only God can make me like God.

You may find yourself wondering how I could possibly find anything distasteful about this verse. The quick answer is: the problem is the verb. There are three characteristics worth commenting on, but it's only the third which bothers me.

Firstly, the verb is passive—"we are being transformed"—and I am grateful for that. It means in the last analysis that I do not change myself, but I am changed. Transformation is something done to me. Not that I don't have to cooperate—I do—but this whole thing is God's idea, God's initiative, so I may trust God will do it. Well, that's a relief, anyway.

The second thing is that the verb is present continuous—"we are being transformed." This change is a process, and a long, often arduous process at that. Yet God, who is the one who has decided this is a good idea, is patient and determined. However many years it takes, God will do it. Every circumstance, every crisis, every relationship, every reading of Scripture, every

---

1. The experiment, by psychologist Robert Zajonc, was reported in *The New York Times* in 1987 (Goleman, "Long-Married Couples Do Look Alike," para. 6).

2. The King James Version translated this as "the Spirit of the Lord," which is unremarkable but not entirely accurate. The Revised Standard Version got a little closer by saying, "the Lord who is the Spirit." But even then, they have introduced a couple of words that Paul did not use. The NRSV is perhaps the most accurate by saying simply, "the Lord, the Spirit." This then becomes an important reference when thinking about the doctrine of the Trinity.

3. Smail, *Reflected Glory*, 29. Much of this chapter is dependent on Smail's reading of this text (24–29), which I came across soon after its publication.

worship service, every act of servanthood—anything can contribute to it, as long as I am open to the work of the Lord the Spirit.

Now we come to the heart of what really disturbs me, not just about this verse, but specifically about this verb. Have you figured out what it is? The verb is plural: "we are being transformed." Doesn't that concern you? It should. Frankly, to anyone who has grown up in the Global North in the last 300 years, this goes against everything we have ever been taught.

Think of what was drummed into us from childhood: "Stand up for yourself." "It's a dog-eat-dog world out there." "Look out for number one." "You can make it if you try." "You can't trust anyone these days." "Everything you need you have within." Or think of that folk hero, the Little Red Engine: "I think I can, I think I can, I think I can . . ." and finally he does it, all by himself. And the implication is: if he can do it, so can you—all by yourself.

And now Paul ruins this beautiful verse by pitting it against the accumulated wisdom of the past 300 years. The nerve of the man. It's almost as if he is saying, "This whole transformation project is not going to be possible without other people. If I am truly to become like Jesus, fulfill my potential as a human being in full image of God, what do I need? I need . . . other people." What a letdown. I just find this so discouraging. I don't mind being told I can only do this with God. That's OK. God and I are pretty tight anyway. But now Paul is telling me I can only do this with other people. Frankly, I find it quite offensive.

It gets worse. If it was simply saying I need to draw on other people's resources to become all God wants me to be, that might be OK. The transformation is still something that's happening to me, and the community is secondary. But it's worse than that. The verse begins "we all": in the Greek, neither of those words is grammatically necessary, so they are apparently put in for emphasis—almost as though Paul enjoys this group thing. I begin to wonder if Paul is really interested in me at all. How can I put this? He somehow seems to think the community comes first and the individual second. It's all we, we, we, you, you, you. I guess I didn't usually notice this in the New Testament because English doesn't distinguish between first-person singular and first-person plural—both are simply "you"—so there is no way to know if the reference means me or us.[4]

Now I couldn't help noticing that during this retreat, people got hold of this community idea and began to think of some of the ways people in Christian community can help another grow in the likeness of Christ. Here are some of the things they suggested would be good for this community:

---

4. Michael Griffiths complains that the distinction "is perfectly clear in Greek, Chinese, Japanese or any decent language" (Griffiths, *Cinderella with Amnesia*, 23–35).

- small groups for sharing, Bible study, and prayer;
- spontaneous prayer;
- having supper or coffee together;
- taking initiative to talk to people, not waiting for them to make the first move;
- taking initiative to talk with and help international students;
- respecting others, not judging them at first glance, taking their views seriously, even if they are different from mine;
- cooperation, not competition;
- giving special honor to those who serve, whether janitor, secretary, or college president;
- telling people what you appreciate about them;
- bearing one another's burdens.[5]

You see the problem? These things could take up a lot of time, for one thing. I don't know about you, but I'm here for my studies and then I'm out of here to do real ministry. Isn't that what we're all here for? These ideas could also mean spending time with people who are different from me, who might change my thinking. These ideas could mean making myself vulnerable. They would certainly mean thinking about other people's needs. It could take my time, my energy, my love. My grades could drop. Do you see how dangerous this all is?

Well, if you want to go that route, that's up to you. I'm just warning you—it'll be costly. Sure, Paul thinks this is the only way worth living. Sure, he thinks this is the only way to be a community that reflects the beauty of Jesus, who is the image of God. Sure, he thinks Christians can become a model for the new humanity this way.

But personally, I think it could be the death of you. I'm going to check out the new age section in the bookstore. Anyone coming with me?

---

5. I took this list from newsprint taped to the wall where the items had been listed by the small discussion groups.

5

Redeeming the Idols

Jeremiah 2:12–14

IN THE WYCLIFFE COLLEGE chapel on Thursday mornings, faculty take it in turns to preach their way through a book of the Bible or a theme. This sermon was the first of a series in the Fall of 2015, entitled "Idols of our Time." Why did I get to preach the first in the series? Because I was rash enough to suggest the idea in the first place. That's the way these things go.

There have been many theological influences in my life, one of them the Reformed tradition. Of course, Anglicanism came out of the Protestant Reformation in the sixteenth century, and is the English equivalent of the Reformed churches of Europe, but over the centuries that connection has often been overlooked. In my life, I was introduced to contemporary Reformed thinking by Brian Walsh and Richard Middleton at the University of Toronto in the late 1970s, and it has frequently proved life-giving. This sermon represents one of the many ways it has shaped my thinking.

In 2017, this series of sermons became a book, Confronting the Idols of Our Age.

> Be appalled, O heavens, at this,
> be shocked, be utterly desolate,
> says the Lord,
> for my people have committed two evils:
> they have forsaken me,

> the fountain of living water,
> and dug out cisterns for themselves,
> cracked cisterns
> that can hold no water (Jer 2:12–13).

President Calvin Coolidge was a man of few words. He came home from church one day and his wife asked him what the sermon had been about. He replied, "Sin." His wife (who obviously knew him well) persisted, "And what did he have to say about sin?" The president replied, "He was against it."

Jeremiah is against idolatry. But he says it with a little more passion than Calvin Coolidge. In fact, Jeremiah is absolutely boiling over with outrage. In verse 12 he cries out: "Be appalled, O heavens, at this, be shocked, be utterly desolate, says the Lord." To Jeremiah, this idol worship is beyond comprehension: How can you possibly do this? No other nation has done such a thing. Even though their gods are nothing, at least they're loyal to their gods! And you had so many privileges!

WHO MADE THE IDOLS?

So . . . I have two shocking statements for you this morning. Shocking statement number one: an idol is a good thing. How can it possibly be good? Because God created it. After all, nothing exists that God did not create and God created all things good. Thus sex can be an idol, but before it was an idol it was a good creation of God. Materialism is an idol, but to have a material world was God's idea in the first place. Workaholism is an idol, but work is itself a good gift of God.

What turns these good gifts of God into idols is what we have done with them. We have removed them from under the authority of God, where they could have been channels of God's blessing to us. We have also stopped exercising our own God-delegated authority over them—which was a part of our God-given stewardship of the world.

Instead, we have put these things on a pedestal and made them into mini-gods. We have given them power over our lives that they were not created to have and which (note this) they are not capable of bearing. As Paul puts it, we "worship the creature (the created thing) instead of the Creator" (Rom 1:25). If you like, we are putting Saul's armor on David and finding he cannot bear the weight. David is a great shepherd boy, but he is useless as a knight in shining armor.

Why do we do this foolish thing? Jeremiah pinpoints the problem in verse 20: "Long ago you broke your yoke, and burst your bonds, and you said, 'I will not serve!'" (In saying this he anticipates Milton's Satan: "Better to reign in Hell than serve in Heaven."[1]) The first taste of this is in the garden, when the serpent promises: "You will be as gods" (Gen 3:5). You do not need God: you can be your own god. There is the first idol: us. Ultimately, that is why we like idols: because they help prop up our own idolatry, and perpetuate our illusion that we are in control.

But of course, human beings are already as God-like as they are capable of being, since they are in the image of God. God has blessed us with all the godness we can handle. And so, when human beings try to play God, they get into trouble because the job is way above their pay grade.

So what is the attraction of idols? For one thing, idols are less demanding than God. They make wonderful promises: they will make you happy, they will solve your problems, and they will give your life meaning and purpose. And because God has given them only limited power—they are creatures as we are—we think they are easier to control, easier to bend to our will than Almighty God.

The trouble is that, in the end, our idols cannot keep their promises, and they will destroy us. As Jeremiah says, the people "went after worthless things, and became worthless themselves" (2:5). If we are looking to David in Saul's armor to win our battles, the Philistines will destroy us.

Part of their destructiveness comes from the fact that we are created to become like the things we worship. "Those who make [idols] are like them; so are all who trust in them" (Ps 115:8). We are made to worship God and to become like God. That is our high destiny. So, if we worship lesser things, we will become less than God intends for us.

Jeremiah has a powerful image for all this, that of water: "My people have committed two evils: they have forsaken me, the fountain of living water, and dug out cisterns for themselves, cracked cisterns that can hold no water" (13). In that culture, the people would build big water tanks to catch the rain in the rainy season so they would have a water supply in times of drought. So to have a leaky cistern was a disaster! No water, no life. It's as simple as that.

Rick Warren imagines it this way:

> It's like this. We're hopelessly lost in the desert, dying of thirst, seeking anything to quench our parched, dry throats. We see a kiosk with big flashing neon lights, and God is holding up a sign that says, "Living Water Available Here." Yet we say, "No, thanks, God! Appreciate the offer, but I see a shovel over there. I think I'll dig my own cistern!"

---

1. Milton, *Paradise Lost*, 13.

Off we trot to start digging our own well and our own cistern. We abandon God—who does not just have water but a *spring* of water that will never dry up—and we decide to figure our problem out by ourselves.

The problem is our cisterns always break; they never hold up. The water leaks out, so we remain thirsty, unable to quench our own thirst.[2]

As Jeremiah says: "In the time of their trouble they say, 'Come and save us!' But where are your gods that you made for yourself? Let them come, if they can save you, in your time of trouble" (2:27–28). The idols let us down precisely when we need them most.

Every way of life has its own distinctive temptations to idolatry. Here is an example from one world which people here this morning know well: that of theological seminary. The academic study of theology is a good thing, a gift of the Creator. It is a thing to love, revel in, and find delight in. So how does it become an idol? Do you know the phrase, "iatrogenic disease?" An iatrogenic disease is one which you catch in hospital. You go into hospital with appendicitis and while you are there you catch C. difficile. If you had not gone to hospital, you would not have caught it. In the same way there are diseases that can only be caught in seminary. As John Calvin famously said: "[Human] nature is a perpetual factory of idols"[3]—and that factory does not cease production just because someone enters seminary.

So how does studying theology (of all things) carry the danger of idolatry? Surely religious pursuits are immune from such a worldly danger! But the study of theology can become idolatrous in the same way any good thing becomes an idol: when it gets taken from under the lordship of Jesus and becomes a god in its own right; when it becomes an end in itself rather than a means to an end, the appropriate end of all human life, serving God more effectively.

I remember a preacher saying, "It was such a thrill the first time I said in a sermon, 'In the Greek it says . . .'" But what exactly is the thrill in this? Is it that, if I tell them "the Greek," the congregation will be better equipped to serve God? That is quite possible. Or is the thrill that they will be impressed with me and my learning? Will it help them look through me to God, or will quoting the Greek cause their gaze to stop with me? Is it about God, or about me? If it is about me, it is an idol.

---

2. Warren, cited in Haystack Bible Commentary, "Jer 2:13," paras. 3–5.
3. Calvin, *Institutes*, 1:108.

CAN IDOLS BE REDEEMED?

What then should be done with an idol? Here's the second shocking statement: God can redeem idols. I do not mean "redeem" in the sense that human beings are redeemed: that through the cross of Jesus our sins are forgiven, we are reconciled to God, and we find our proper place in God's world. Rather, I mean an idol can be restored to its proper place in God's created order, whether it be our attitude to sex, to material things, to work—or to the academic study of theology.

How does that redemption happen? When those who practice idolatry repent and literally change their minds. They confess: "I realize this thing is not the most important thing in the world, this thing is not going to give me meaning and purpose and identity. This thing is a leaky cistern. What I need is living water! And only God can supply that." As part of surrendering their life to God in Christ, they hand over that idol to the God who made it and who wants to remake it. They take the armor off David and let him be himself—a capable shepherd boy with five smooth stones and a sling.

It may be that Jesus was thinking of Jeremiah when he talked about water. He says to the woman at the well:

> If you knew the gift of God, and who it is that is saying to you, 'Give me a drink,' you would have asked him, and he would have given you living water. . . . Everyone who drinks of this water [in Jeremiah's terms, the idols] will be thirsty again, but those who drink of the water that I will give them will never be thirsty. The water that I will give will become in them a spring of water gushing up to eternal life." (John 4:10, 13–14).

There is a place in C. S. Lewis's *Prince Caspian* where Lucy and Susan are with Aslan, the lion who is the Christ-figure, and they encounter Bacchus, the god of wine, fertility, and theatre (among other things), and a multitude of his followers. He is said to symbolize "everything which is chaotic, dangerous and unexpected, everything which escapes human reason." And a wild party ensues. When it is all over, Susan says, "I wouldn't have felt safe with Bacchus and all his wild girls if we'd met them without Aslan." And Lucy replies, "I should think not."[4]

Lewis is expressing his deep conviction that everything in creation—including those things which we so easily turn into idols—finds its rightful place only when it comes under the lordship of Christ. Apart from Jesus, those things are not safe. They can destroy us. With him, they bring life and joy, as their Creator intended.

---

4. Lewis, *Prince Caspian*, 138.

6

God is Always Bigger

WE ARRIVED IN CANADA on August 22nd, 1977, and lived for the first four years on the second floor of a house on Huron Street in Toronto. The house was owned by my employer, InterVarsity Christian Fellowship of Canada, as a center for student activity. When we looked around for a church to join, the closest one (five minutes' walk, which was a factor since we had small children) was Knox Presbyterian Church. We became good friends with the College and Career pastor and his wife, and under their leadership the church had developed a thriving student ministry.

Over the years since then, Knox has been utterly amazing in the degree of faithful prayer and financial support they have given to our ministry. It's a very long time since 1977! After we moved to Ottawa in 1982, I was still invited back as a guest preacher from time to time, most frequently for their annual Student Welcome Sunday in September. This is one of those sermons, from September, 2008.

My wife, Deborah, became a Christian at Oxford University many years ago. One of her chief fears was that within a year she would understand all there was to know about Christianity and she would be bored. Suffice it to say, that was not the case, and to this day she continues to learn and grow and be stretched about what it means to be a Christian and to follow Jesus.

Why? Because God was bigger than she thought. You may remember that scene in *The Last Battle*, the last of the Narnia stories, where the children enter a small, dirty stable, and to their amazement find inside "blue sky overhead [and] the grassy country spreading out as far as [they] could see in every direction." Prince Tirian says, "the Stable seen from within and the Stable seen from without are two different places." And Digory replies, "Yes . . . Its inside is bigger than its outside."[1]

And I hope that if you have been a follower of Jesus for any length of time, that that has been your experience too—that the inside of Christian faith has proved bigger than it once appeared on the outside. As the apostle Paul says, "Thanks be to God for his indescribable gift" (2 Cor 9:15). Apparently, the literal meaning of "indescribable" is "not yet fully drawn out," thus, "Thanks be to God for his not-yet-fully-drawn out" gift. There is always more to be drawn out: God is bigger than we thought, bigger than we think.

I don't need to tell you that the experience of being a Christian is not all sweetness and light. Sometimes the outside of the stable, although it looked small, actually seemed brighter and more attractive than the inside turned out to be, however large it may be, and it can be tempting to go back. God is bigger than we thought—but we don't necessarily like that "bigger."

If you are like me, there have been times when our experience of the Christian life is disillusioning, times when we experience "Disappointment with God," as Philip Yancey bluntly puts it.[2] We're embarrassed to come out and say it, because it seems blasphemous and people might think we're losing our faith. You probably know the kind of thing I mean.

In particular, the Christian life gets tough when things go wrong. Here are some examples that occur to me—but I'm pretty sure it's not just me:

Prayers are not answered—and there seems absolutely no reason why. I'm not talking about trivial, selfish prayers, where it's easy to see why they might not be answered. I'm talking about serious, unselfish prayers, prayed with as much faith and passion as we can manage.

People get sick and die: young people, healthy people, people we love, people we need, people the church needs, people with so much potential, people we have been praying will become Christians and they haven't. And it feels kind of wimpy to say, "Well, I guess God has his reasons," or "God knows what he's doing"—you know the kind of thing people say. In what sense is this the act of a loving God? I think of a single mother with two teenage daughters in my own church who took her own life and was found

---

1. Lewis, *Last Battle*, 133–34.
2. Yancey, *Disappointment with God*.

by one of her daughters when she came home from school. As my pastor said, "I know God gives us free will to do these things, but . . ." And he didn't finish the sentence. He didn't need to.

In recent years, I have done some research to find out what drove people away from church. One of the most common answers was disillusionment with church. Churches that preach grace but practice law. Churches where there was financial impropriety. Churches where leaders were caught in sexual sin. Of course, theologically we know churches are full of sinners like you and me, so it's not surprising, but at the same time we secretly ask ourselves, "Is this the best God can do with people who claim to be following Jesus?"

Another thing I noticed in my research was that the same people who got disillusioned with Christians also discovered so-called non-Christians who were actually very nice people—decent, compassionate, respectful, thoughtful, and generous—often more so than those within the church. They were not at all the terrible sinners they had sometimes been warned were lurking outside the walls of the church. And they thought, "This is not the way I thought God organized the world. Something is wrong with this picture."

I could go on: you don't have to be a Christian very long to have this kind of experience—or a hundred like them—and to ask these questions. And the biggest question of all we find ourselves asking is: Where is God in all this? Or even more searchingly: God doesn't seem to be as I thought, so then, who or what exactly is God, after all?

As I think of my own life, there were three particular experiences that shook my faith:

- One was many years ago, when Deborah and I felt God was asking us to have a student live with us as part of our family: she was brilliant, troubled, and not very strong in her faith. We confidently expected God would use us to strengthen her in her faith. But after eighteen months in our home, during which we worked very hard to help her, she announced that she could no longer call herself a Christian, and moved out. And we asked: "God, what happened here? We thought you had set this up. What went wrong?" And to say, "Well, God gives people free will" didn't answer anything and wasn't very comforting. Was God different from how we had thought?

- Another was the death of a young IVCF staff member I had been mentoring, Mike Hare, in a car crash in February of 1989. He was young, bright, passionate for Christ, and a winsome evangelist. He had been married for eighteen months, and his wife, Catherine, had recently had their first child. That weekend, he was driving a group of students to an evangelistic ski weekend in the Grey-Bruce area. The van he was driving hit a ridge of snow, and crossed the median into the face of an oncoming truck, and that was that. "God, what just happened here? Why was that ridge of snow there? Why was that truck there at just that moment? Couldn't you have held it back for just ten seconds? And now what? What about Catherine and her baby?" And again the question: So, if this kind of thing can happen, what is God like?

- A third has been the experience of seeing people, mature Christians, often in leadership, simply walk away from Christian faith and church. Perhaps the most famous Canadian example was Charles Templeton, a fine evangelist who had been mentored by Billy Graham. And we find ourselves asking: "God, what went wrong here? What destroyed their faith? Was it their fault, or did you somehow let them down? Who exactly are you, God?"

Perhaps because of these experiences, I went through a period of about three years when God simply wasn't real. The Bible and prayer and worship were dry as dust. I didn't give up being a Christian, but I might have called myself a Christian agnostic—that is, a Christian who doesn't know very much. At one point, there were only three things I was sure of in my faith: that God created a good world (it didn't happen by chance), that Jesus had come, lived, died, and risen again (I couldn't deny those things), and that at the end of time, God would straighten everything out (it seemed to follow from the other two). I clung to those three things.

So what does one do with this kind of experience? How does one understand it? Indeed, is it possible to understand it at all? I can understand why some just walk away from Christian faith.

I think some measure of understanding is possible, and I call as my star witness C. S. Lewis. You may know that he didn't marry until he was in his fifties. Then his wife, Joy, got cancer, and wasn't expected to live. In fact, she made a miraculous recovery—at least, Lewis and Joy believed it was a miracle—and they lived happily together for three years. Then the cancer unexpectedly returned, and six months later Joy died.

Lewis kept a journal during the first weeks and months after Joy died, and it was eventually published as *A Grief Observed*. Although he is describing his reactions to his wife's death, I think many of us feel and think as he did, even if our crises are less than the death of a spouse.

The first stage of his writing expresses his anger and confusion towards God. If God lets this kind of thing happen, how can God be called good?

Sooner or later I must face the question in plain language. What reason have we, except our own desperate wishes, to believe that God is, by any standard we can conceive, "good"? Doesn't all the prima facie evidence suggest exactly the opposite? What have we to set against it? We set Christ against it. But what if he were mistaken? Almost his last words may have a perfectly clear meaning. He had found that the Being he called Father was horribly and infinitely different from the way he had supposed. The trap, so long and carefully prepared and so subtly baited, was at last sprung, in the cross. The vile practical joke had succeeded. What chokes every prayer and every hope is the memory of all the prayers [Joy] and I offered and all the false hopes we had. Not hopes raised merely by our own wishful thinking; hopes encouraged, even forced upon us, by false diagnoses, by X-ray photographs, by strange remissions, by one temporary recovery that might have been ranked as a miracle. Step by step we were led "up the garden path." Time after time, when he seemed most gracious he was really preparing the next torture.[3]

Do you ever feel that way? But as time passes, Lewis's attitude changes. He realizes it's not rational to think of God as evil, as the Cosmic Sadist, because evil could never create "love, or laughter, or daffodils, or a frosty sunset."[4] He finds the doors of heaven are not bolted against him after all. He gets a sense that his wife is still alive in God's presence. And as he reflects back on his spiritual journey through grief, he thinks he sees part of what has been happening to him. God, he says, is not the Cosmic Sadist, but perhaps the Great Iconoclast instead:

> My idea of God is not a divine idea. It has to be shattered time after time. He shatters it Himself. He is the great iconoclast. Could we not almost say that this shattering is one of the marks of His presence? The Incarnation is the supreme example; it leaves all previous ideas of the Messiah in ruins.[5]

We are used to thinking of God in certain ways: God loves us, God guides us, God provides for us, God forgives us. All true. But do we think of God as one who destroys our images of God? Probably not as often.

But why would God want to destroy our images of him? Surely, since God dwells in unapproachable light, we need images. You can't think of God without an image. If we try, we end up thinking of God as "a vast tapioca

3. Lewis, *Grief Observed*, 26–27.
4. Lewis, *Grief Observed*, 27.
5. Lewis, *Grief Observed*, 52.

pudding"[6] (as Lewis says elsewhere). So what's the problem? Why does God want to destroy our images?

Here, I think, is the key. Psalm 115:18 says: "Those who worship idols become like them." Those who worship idols become like them. God is opposed to the worship of idols—that's not news to any reader of the Old Testament. But have you ever wondered exactly why God opposes idols? It's not because he's jealous in the obvious sense.

Let's come at it like this. What is God up to in your life and mine? What is God hoping for, aiming for? I think you can summarize it by saying, God wants to form us to be like Jesus. Or, to put it another way, God wants to restore the image of God in us that has been spoiled through sin. And we are to be like Jesus because Jesus "is the image of the invisible God" (Col 1:15). He shows us what a human being perfectly in the image of God looks like. So God wants us to be God-like. Why? So we can be all that God longs for us to be, become the person God created us to be from the beginning. Because God loves us.

Our imagination is always dreaming up images of God that are not God. And this is dangerous because, as the psalmist knew, we become like the things we worship. So if we are worshiping an image of God that is less than God—which all images will be—then God in mercy has to break those images. Otherwise, we are going to grow into a distorted and inadequate image of God, instead of growing into the image of God himself.

I think this is what has happened to me through the difficulties I told you about earlier. My image of God wasn't adequate. It didn't make sense of the things I was experiencing. And that image broke. The pattern has repeated itself time and time again. And each time the image gets broken, I realize God is bigger than I thought, more mysterious than I thought, more uncontrollable than I think I hoped. Aslan is not a tame lion.

I suppose God in mercy will continue that process until we die and see God face to face—when we will realize how puny and inadequate all our images were, compared to the incomparable beauty of God. Or, to put it another way, there is a scene in *Prince Caspian* where Lucy meets Aslan after a year away from Narnia, and she says to him: "Aslan . . . you're bigger." And he replies, "That is because you are older, little one." "Not because you are?" asks Lucy. "I am not. But every year you grow, you will find me bigger."[7]

Not a bad prayer, is it? That, every year we grow, we may find God bigger.

---

6. Lewis, *Miracles*, 78.

7. Lewis, *Prince Caspian*, 124.

B

Facets of Spirituality

I'M NOT SURE WHEN the word "spirituality" became the common term it is today. I do remember that Jim Berney, when he was President of Inter-Varsity Canada in the 1980s and 1990s, started including reflections on "spirituality" in his regular newsletters to staff, and people saying with some suspicion, "Spirituality? What's that?" Now it has become so common that we wonder how we managed without it. Of course, popular usage also means an increasing range of meanings. Spirituality? What's that? Here I am using it to mean simply "those things that nurture our spiritual lives." For Christians, that means specifically "nurturing our spiritual lives as disciples of Jesus."

7

Five Spiritualities in the Body of Christ

This is the text of a plenary talk I gave in May of 2011, at an Anglican clergy conference in the Diocese of Ontario, based in Kingston, at the invitation of my friend, the then-bishop, Peter Mason. Clergy conferences of most denominations include people with a range of theologies and spiritualities. This may be particularly true for Anglicans! Since I am a card-carrying evangelical, though of a fairly broad-minded type—when you put "Anglican" and "evangelical" together, that's what generally happens—I wanted to address a topic that would draw people together, and not further polarities.

Those familiar with Richard Foster's Streams of Living Water *(2001) will recognize the strong influence of that book, with its division of Christian spiritualities into Contemplative, Holiness, Charismatic, Social Justice, Evangelical, and Incarnational. I have omitted the Holiness stream for the sake of simplicity and brevity. Make of that what you will.*

Once upon a time, there were five nice Christians who lived in the same city but had never met one another. Let me introduce you to them. I'll tell you a little about each, and then I have three questions to ask of each one.

1. COLIN CONTEMPLATIVE

Even as a child, Colin loved to go for walks by himself. He learned at an early age that God could be his friend, and he loved to talk with this friend as he walked. As a result, when he grew up and told his parents he wanted to become a monk, they were not taken by surprise. Colin loves the life of the monastery: the extended periods of silence, the regular times of prayer, chanting the whole psalter every month, and the hard work in the fields. He also acts as a spiritual director for four or five layfolk who come to see him on a monthly basis. He would be very surprised to know this, but they are a little in awe of the strength of his spiritual life and what they feel to be his intimate knowledge of God.

- My first question for Colin is: How does he know God? He replies with quiet confidence, "God is to be known in silence and contemplation." He likes to quote Mother Theresa: "In prayer, sometimes I tell him I love him, sometimes he tells me he loves me, and sometimes neither of us says anything."

- For my second question, I ask: Where do you believe the kingdom is? He smiles. "The kingdom of God is within, to be discovered and explored in relationship with God, who is the King."

- Question 3: Is there a particular verse from the Bible that inspires and guides you? Again, he doesn't hesitate: "Be still and know that I am God."

2. THEN THERE IS ASTRID SOCIAL-ACTIVIST

Astrid was actually born Astrid Activist, but then she married Steve Social, so she became Astrid Social-Activist. Astrid grew up in the church, but God had never been particularly real to her until one Victoria Day weekend her youth group went to a conference where Shane Claiborne was speaking. There for the first time she understood the heart of God identifies in a special way with the weak, the poor, and the oppressed of the world. It was a revelation to her—and a revolution in her understanding of the Christian faith. She left the rather conventional, middle-class church of her parents out in the suburbs, and started attending a downtown church that had a wide range of social programs.

- So, Astrid, I want to know: How do you know God? She answers at once: "I see the face of God in the face of the poor."

- And, Astrid, Where is the kingdom of God? "The kingdom won't come," she replies, "until the structures of society are reformed so that power and wealth are justly distributed in our world, where nobody goes hungry, where all have dignity and fulfilling work. That would be the *shalom* of God."
- And a favorite Scripture? It's in Matthew 25: "Just as you did it to one of the least of these who are members of my family, you did it to me."

Next I would like you to meet:

3. EDDIE EVANGELICAL

The most important day in Eddie's life was the day he went forward at a Billy Graham rally in Toronto to indicate that he wanted to accept Jesus Christ as his personal Savior. From that day on everything has been different for Eddie. He joined a church where he feels the Bible is faithfully taught. He reads the Bible and prays every day, and tries to follow what he learns there. He goes to a midweek Bible study group where people sing and share, study Scripture together, and pray for one another. Eddie is a clerk in a law firm, and he does his job well, trying to be a good witness for Jesus by his conscientious work and his good humor, and, whenever he has a chance, he talks about his faith in Jesus.

- So, I ask him, Eddie, how do you know God? His face lights up as he replies: "I know God through his word. He speaks to me and I try to listen and obey."
- And the kingdom, Eddie? What is the kingdom? He replies with passion, "When every man and woman has acknowledged the lordship of Jesus Christ in their lives: that's the kingdom."
- Choosing a favorite verse is harder for Eddie. He can't decide between 2 Timothy 3:16, "All Scripture is inspired by God and profitable for training, for reproof, for correction and for training in righteousness," and, on other days, the great commission of Matthew 28: "Go, make disciple of all nations." Both are very central to Eddie's understanding of what it means to be a follower of Jesus.

My next friend is:

4. CHRIS CHARISMATIC

Chris would describe his faith like this: "I had been a Christian for some years, but somehow I had never known much about the Holy Spirit. It was as though I believed in a Holy Binity rather than a Holy Trinity." Then one evening, some friends of Chris dragged him off against his will to a service at the Airport Christian Fellowship in Toronto. There Chris was prayed for, was "slain in the Spirit," as the terminology goes, and, from that night on, his outlook on the Christian life was quite different. Although he hasn't given up on his high Anglican church on Sundays, he goes to an interdenominational prayer group during the week, where there is lively worship and speaking in tongues, and where the sick are prayed for and sometimes dramatically healed. Chris is praying his priest will discover what he has found; the priest meanwhile is praying Chris won't go over the edge—though he's not quite sure what that edge might be.

- So what does it mean to you to know God, Chris? He smiles and says, "Easy: in Spirit-filled worship, that's where I feel God and I see God."
- And what for you is the kingdom? "No question: 'the kingdom of God does not consist in talk but in power' (1 Cor 4:20): wherever the Spirit is free to work, that's where the kingdom is."
- His favorite verse, not surprisingly, at least since that fateful night at the airport, is Acts 1:8: "You shall receive power when the Holy Spirit comes upon you."

Last and by no means least is:

5. SAMANTHA SACRAMENTAL

Samantha returned to church in her late thirties after the breakup of her marriage. She came in the first place because she needed the spiritual strength the church seemed to offer, but to her surprise it was actually the beauty and the mystery of the Eucharist that drew her and fascinated her. After a couple of years, her priest encouraged her to think about ordination, and, as she began to study theology, she came to understand more of why she loved the sacraments: it was the sense that the God who had been present in the human form of Jesus was also the God who was present in bread and wine, and was also the God who was present everywhere, making all of life sacred. That understanding began to transform her whole life, and breathed life into everything she did, even the most menial tasks. The sacrament on Sundays was a reminder that the other six days of the week were also sacramental. The sacramental nature of the six days focused and found its fulfillment for her in the sacrament at the altar.

- So where do you know God, Samantha? "I know God most intimately in the Eucharist."
- And the kingdom? "Well, in a sense, the kingdom is everywhere because all of life is God's, but in the Eucharist the reality of the kingdom is made visible in bread and wine."
- And do you have a favorite Bible verse? "Sure, at the end of the Emmaus Road story in Luke 24: 'He was known to them in the breaking of the bread.'"

Now my guess is that you have met all of these five at different points in your life. My guess too is you feel closer to one or even two of these than you do to the others. (I think it's unlikely anyone will feel an equal affinity for all five—but I could be wrong!)

Now I probably don't need to tell you that there have been times when these five have been mortal enemies. In fact, I deliberately didn't tell you what each of these characters thinks of the others, but I have to confess that some of them don't have a very high opinion of some of the others. There have been times in living memory when a church has gone from, let us say, Anglo-Catholic to evangelical (or vice versa) and half the congregation has left, while the other half has gritted its teeth and said, "We can outlast whoever the bishop throws at us. And, if necessary, we can even outlast the bishop."

There have been times when contemplatives have felt pity for the noisiness and superficial piety of the charismatics, and times when evangelicals have felt that social activists lacked spiritual depth. (I am putting these criticisms in polite language, you understand.) The list could go on: after all, each of the five would have criticisms of each of the other four, and that would make twenty points—but you can probably figure out what they would be, and we have more important things to think about!

I want to argue, however, that there is strength in each one of these, and that we need each of these traditions.

One reason I think that is because each of these is clearly rooted in Scripture and in Christian tradition. Let me illustrate. It just so happened that our five friends (friends with us, that is: not necessarily friends with each other) were at a diocesan conference on spirituality (these things happen all over the place, you understand) and that, at the beginning of the day, the reading during worship was from Acts 10, Peter's speech to Cornelius.

Listen to what it says:

> You know the message God sent to the people of Israel, preaching peace by Jesus Christ—he is Lord of all. (36)

Colin Contemplative heard that sentence and nodded gravely. *There it is,* he thought, *the message of peace. That's what it's all about: peace with God, peace with one another, peace with the world.* And if he had not been feeling particularly gracious, he might have thought, *I hope these other folk are listening.* But, actually, he was feeling gracious. As for the other folk, well, they were listening, but they didn't hear what he heard.

The reader hadn't stopped:

> That message spread throughout Judea . . . how God anointed Jesus of Nazareth with the Holy Spirit and with power; how he went about doing good and healing all who were oppressed by the devil, for God was with him. (38)

And Chris Charismatic suddenly sat up straight, and surreptitiously looked around to see if his priest had been convicted by that powerful sentence.

Now it came to pass that Chris happened to be sitting next to Astrid (whom he hadn't met yet), and she just happened to notice something different in the same sentence that she felt was just for her: "Jesus of Nazareth went about doing good." *That's what it's all about,* she thought: *he went about doing good.* In her more cynical moments, she felt most Christians just "went about": Jesus, however, went about doing good. Why didn't they get it?

But the reader hadn't finished:

> We are witnesses to all he did, both in Judea and Jerusalem. (39)

Now it was Eddie Evangelical's turn: *Ooh, witnessing,* he thought. *That's what we need round here: real witnessing. Telling people what we know about Jesus. You don't have to be a great preacher to do that.*

And Samantha? You won't be surprised to know she wasn't disappointed either:

> They put him to death . . . but God raised him on the third day and allowed him to appear . . . to us . . . who ate and drank with him after he rose from the dead. (41)

There's the Eucharist right there, she thought: *eating and drinking with Jesus after he rose from the dead. I could preach on that tomorrow,* she thought (since she hadn't quite got her sermon together yet).

You see what I mean? Each of these types, at its best, seeks to know Jesus Christ, to be faithful to him, to know him, love him, serve him. Each of these is a way of being faithful to our Christian heritage. And each of these is a way to grow into all that God has in mind for us. Yet each does it in a different way:

The strength of the contemplative is to know God in quietness and silence, and to call the church back to that.

The strength of the social activist is to challenge the comfortable middle-class assumptions of the church, and to remind us of the uncomfortable truth that though God loves all people, God has a bias towards the poor—just as you might love all your children equally, but if one is in pain or difficulty, your heart goes out to that one first.

The evangelical shames us by his enthusiasm for the gospel of Jesus (very un-Canadian), and by his knowledge of the Bible (very un-Anglican), and by his warm spontaneous praying (very nonliturgical). Maybe he too knows something we don't.

The charismatic holds our feet to the fire, and says, *Every Sunday you say you believe in the Holy Spirit, but in reality you are more worried about whether the Spirit comes from the Father and the Son or from the Father alone than you do about allowing the Holy Spirit to come at all! Hey, get with the program!*

And the sacramental says, *Do you realize that God may be known in all of life? You say "he became incarnate by the Virgin Mary," but do you realize what that means? That there is no longer any division between sacred and secular?*

My question would be: Which of those emphases can the church do without? Which one can we dare to be without?

Of course, you may argue each has its weaknesses, or potential weaknesses, and that is perfectly true. I'm quite sure none of these weaknesses would be true of any of the representatives of these five streams here today, so nobody should feel got at, but nevertheless:

Colin Contemplative may sometimes forget it is possible to know God in the middle of a traffic jam, or while changing a baby's diaper, or even at a riotous party.

Astrid Social-Activist can get so wrapped up in her social concerns that she forgets the Jesus who inspired her in the first place.

Eddie Evangelical can end up treating people as one-dimensional souls needing to be saved rather than people who are body, mind, emotions, and soul in community, in the image of God.

Ironically enough, Chris Charismatic can actually end up putting the Holy Spirit in a box—this is where the Spirit is, this is what will cause the Spirit to act, this is what enables the Spirit to work. Forgetting that the

Holy Spirit is the Third Person of the Eternal Trinity and that Aslan is not a tame lion.

And Samantha Sacramental can get so wrapped up in the details of doing everything exactly right that she forgets Jesus was the friend of sinners, had messy friendships with messy people who lived messy lives, and is the Jesus who is there at the heart of the Eucharist she loves.

All five of our friends can become pretty legalistic—these are the rules for doing it the Right Way, which just happens to be my way. All of them can become so wrapped up in their distinctive religious stuff that they forget the Jesus who inspired them in the first place. And all of them can reduce the grandeur of the Christian message to something trivial and unworthy.

C. S. Lewis believed the devil didn't have a sense of humor so, if we have a sense of humor, we know where it must come from. I don't know about you, but sometimes God's sense of humor seems a little, what shall we say, dry, so it seemed like rather a twisted kind of joke when the conference divided into table groups for discussion, and (by a strange coincidence) Colin, Astrid, Eddie, Chris, and Samantha ended up in the same discussion group. It didn't take them long to figure out where each was coming from—the name tags were a dead giveaway. Fortunately, the questions they were given headed off some potential nastiness at the pass.

Question 1 was: say something about your tradition of Christian spirituality which might make someone from another tradition want to try it. And question 2 was: Choose one thing you think you could benefit from in one of the other streams of Christian spirituality. There was silence at the table for what felt like a very long time.

Finally, Eddie said: "I have to say I think one of the best things in my tradition is my small group Bible study. It's become an amazing support group for me: there's warmth and laughter and prayer in the group, and we feel the presence of Jesus right there, and I wouldn't miss it for anything."

The others looked thoughtful. Then Astrid said, "Maybe I could check it out one of these Wednesdays. To be honest, I sometimes get very drained in my work with street people and advocacy groups, and I would love to have a Christian support group like that. Do you think that would be OK? They wouldn't try to get me 'born again?'" Eddie looked earnest: "It'd be OK. I'd protect you."

Chris was next. "I know sometimes our enthusiasm is, well, just that— enthusiasm—and it's not always the Holy Spirit. But I've also known some times when the Spirit really is present but the experience is very gentle and quiet and nonthreatening. And I think anyone could benefit from that. And as for the other question, I think I've got kinda cut off from God's heart for the poor. So, Astrid, maybe I could come with you one of these Saturday nights when you go and give out sandwiches and coffee to street people. Maybe the Holy Spirit will be there too!" She nodded, pleased but a little nervous.

Then Colin chipped in. "Chris, what you just said about the Holy Spirit: I've never heard a charismatic talk that way. I thought it was all noise and drama and showiness. I never thought I could find myself at home in a charismatic meeting, but if I could come with you, I think I'd like to try it. And, as for a strength, I have space for someone to come for spiritual direction. I really think it's something my tradition has to offer, if you don't think that's presumptuous of me to say so."

Samantha responded immediately. "I have to confess that the life has been going out of my relationship with God recently, even at the altar. I still feel badly about how I snapped at the president of the Altar Guild last week. She almost cried. I've been thinking for some time that maybe what I need is some spiritual direction to keep me fresh in my ministry. I think the fact that you're here means I should take you up on your offer."

Chris chuckled. "That's the Holy Spirit: see?"

But Samantha went on. "And as for something to offer: I do think the Eucharist is a window through which to marvel at the activity of God in the world. I don't know how other Christians survive without it!"

Eddie shrugged. "OK, I'll come clean. I've never understood why communion is so important to you people, but the way you talk about it makes me feel I must be missing out. I'd better not start coming to your church or my pastor will get mad at me, but maybe you could suggest a couple of books for me to read."

"Glad to," replied Samantha.

Then the emcee called them to Eucharist, and, to their surprise, they found they wanted to sit together for the service. And, when the Passing of the Peace came, they hugged each other, and some found they had tears in their eyes.

> Now there are varieties of gifts, but the same Spirit; and there are varieties of services but the same Lord; and there are varieties of activities, but it is the same God who activates all of them in everyone. To each is given the manifestation of the Spirit for the common good (1 Cor 12:4–7).

8

Ignatius for Non-Catholics?

When I taught at Wycliffe College, there was a weekly newsletter for the community, called The Morning Star. (John Wycliffe was known as "the morning star of the Reformation," hence the name.) It was mainly for communicating news and announcements for the community in the coming week, but each week faculty and staff took it in turns to write a short, front-page editorial. Sometimes these would follow a theme for a few weeks, but many were just free-standing items of interest to the writer. Several of these are included in this book. This one is from the Fall of 2011, on a topic arising from my own recent experience. This version is somewhat longer, and was published in The Niagara Anglican, *newspaper of the Anglican diocese in which I live, in the summer of 2019.*

If Ignatius Loyola enters our awareness at all, it is likely as head of the pope's anti-Reformation shock troops in the sixteenth century. Like most one-line characterizations, however, that is a caricature. Ignatius (1491–1556) was certainly the founder of the Jesuits, perhaps the most powerful Roman Catholic missionary movement ever. There were certainly Jesuits at the Council of Trent (1545–1563), which set out to combat Protestant "heresies" (though he would not have used quotation marks). And, equally true, we do know that at least once Loyola engaged in debate with Protestants.

But if that were all, we might be forgiven for forgetting the name. His legacy, however, is actually deeper and wider than that, whether we consider ourselves Catholic, Protestant, Anglican, or Anabaptist.

The story is this. Having grown up in Spain, at the age of thirty, Ignatius was wounded in battle against the French. While recovering, there being nothing more interesting to read, he read a life of Christ and a book about the saints—always a dangerous thing to do—and, somewhat like one of his heroes, St. Francis, had a mystical conversion experience. As C. S. Lewis complained, "A young man who wishes to remain a sound Atheist cannot be too careful of his reading. There are traps everywhere."[1] Loyola's life was never the same again. The year was 1531.

Quite soon, he found that people started coming to him for spiritual advice and direction, and discovered he had a gift in this area. Over time, his direction evolved into a more or less standard form now known as the "Spiritual Exercises" of Ignatius Loyola, based on how he had experienced God's work in his own life. Gradually, some friends to whom he had given the exercises, and who had been dramatically affected by them, grew into a group of between six and ten men (yes, they were all men) who lived together and engaged in a ministry of preaching, catechism, and care for the poor. In 1537, this group decided to call themselves the Companions of Jesus. In 1540, the Society of Jesus was given the pope's official approval, and (not surprisingly) Loyola was elected Superior.

Not that all was straightforward, however: twice, Loyola was imprisoned and brought before the Inquisition, who were suspicious of his teaching. Both times he was acquitted. The Jesuits were often a thorn in the church's side, because while they wanted to stay within the Catholic box, they also insisted on stretching it to its limits. (Need I mention that Pope Francis is a Jesuit?) Loyola died in 1556 and was canonized in 1609, by which time the Jesuits numbered around 15,000 and were at work in countries as widespread as China, Peru, and Ethiopia.

These days, much of the old suspicion between Roman Catholics and other churches has evaporated, thank God, and we are at least more understanding of our differences. While I was at Wycliffe College, Anglican students at Wycliffe and Trinity often took courses at Regis, the Jesuit college in the Toronto School of Theology, and Jesuit students were known to take courses at colleges of other denominations.

One fruit of that greater understanding has been increased non-Catholic interest in the Ignatian Exercises. The best-known way to do the

---

1. Lewis, *Surprised by Joy*, 181.

Exercises is during a forty-day retreat, paralleling Christ's forty days in the wilderness. There are many Catholic retreat centers where you can do this.

"But," I hear you cry, "I don't have forty days to be quiet. Good grief! What do you think I am? A monk or a nun? I have a life, you know!" Loyola foresaw that problem, and figured out a way for "busy people" (who existed in his day too) to do the exercises in the course of everyday life—the so-called "Nineteenth Annotation," since it is in section nineteen of his instructions that Ignatius explains it. This way of doing it involves taking an hour a day, following the course of a liturgical year. I know, I know, an hour a day also sounds like an impossibility. That's what I thought when I did this a few years back—but, you know what?—to my amazement, I found the time. I told my spiritual director I didn't know how I was managing it. She smiled mischievously, and said, "Everyone says that." So don't despair.

Doing the exercises is one way that this obscure figure from almost 500 years ago can help us develop our spirituality. But the challenge—and the invitation—of Ignatian spirituality for non-Catholics goes beyond that. There are four areas in particular where I believe he speaks to us.

One is that the exercises require a close engagement with Scripture. People in mainline denominations have often said to me, "I am embarrassed at how little I know the Bible." Loyola can help. One distinctive of his approach is that the student imagines him or herself in the Bible story, whether it be with the shepherds at the manger, with Jesus as he leaves Nazareth and walks to the Jordan River, or with Mary as she encounters the risen Jesus. Many insights come through this contemplative engagement with Scripture that might never come through academic study alone. Even familiar stories take on new dimensions.

I confess, when the exercises required me to read the Prodigal Son for the third time—yes, the third—I was sceptical: "I saw something new the first two times. Give me a break! Surely there can't possibly be anything else?" But of course, there was. (It became a joke with my spiritual director that every week I would say, "Well, I'd read this story a thousand times, but I saw something new this time.")

Secondly, Ignatius could almost have coined the phrase which these days we tend to associate with evangelicals, though it is not unknown in other traditions: "a personal relationship with Jesus." A few years back, a group of doctoral students were discussing an article critiquing this idea of "a personal relationship with Jesus." The author argued that it was anti-community, simplistic, otherworldly, made faith a private matter, and so on. The students agreed. Then they turned to the professor, a very senior and distinguished academic—and a Jesuit—and asked: "So what did you think of the article?" Without turning a hair, he replied, "I felt very sorry for the author." Classic Jesuitism!

As Ignatius guides us through the Gospels, always the emphasis is on what you might say to Jesus and what he might say to you. Of course, orthodox Catholic that he is, for Ignatius, that "personal relationship" is never free-wheeling like that of some Protestants, but is always securely in the context of God the Trinity (most of Ignatius's mystical visions were of the Trinity), within the discipline of regular attendance at mass, and in line with the teaching of the church. Yet at the heart of the Exercises is a yearning to be a more faithful and dedicated disciple of Jesus, and to learn all he has to teach. It was said of Ignatius, "At this time God treated him as a schoolmaster a boy whom he teaches."[2] That's a good perspective for non-Catholics as we think about what that trendy word, "discipleship," means these days.

Thirdly, the Jesuits have a strong sense of mission. In a time when the church is being called to be more "missional," this is worth considering. Unlike many Orders, the Jesuits did not (and do not) build or live in monasteries. They needed (and need) to be flexible and nimble for the sake of Christ's mission. In a letter in 1549, Loyola wrote that Jesuits needed to have "one foot on the road, ready to hasten from one place to another."[3]

This is why Jesuits developed the discipline known as the Examen: pausing twice during the day (noon and evening) to reflect on God's activity in their lives. Where have I sensed God's presence? Where have I felt God's absence? What is God saying to me through these experiences? This was important enough in Loyola's understanding of spirituality that he counseled the Jesuits that, even if they didn't have time to pray (does that sound familiar?), they should still do the Examen! The Examen enabled them to remain open to the promptings of God's Spirit to pursue new areas for mission, even at short notice.

The heart of Ignatian spirituality therefore is internal, personal, and highly portable—though again, that is not in isolation but is set in the context of worship in community. In a day when we are learning to explore ways of doing church differently, this is a helpful example.

The last point of resonance came home to me in a comment by Loyola's biographer Philip Caraman, that Loyola's "contemporaries . . . saw in him, first and foremost, not a champion of Roman Catholicism, still less a hammer of heretics, but a passionate believer in holiness, reaching out with his whole being towards God."[4] Christians in the Global North are not, on the

2. Purcell, *First Jesuit*, 110.
3. Ignatius of Loyola, *Letters of St. Ignatius of Loyola*, 186–87.
4. Caraman, *Ignatius Loyola*, 200–1.

whole, known for unbridled and passionate enthusiasm in their faith. (They are, however, known for understatement.)

Loyola encourages all of us to recognize God-in-Christ as the center of our faith, to experience the love of God, and to respond with love. Jesus did not come to start a new religion. (There was a perfectly good one close at hand.) Rather, he announced the turning point in God's plan to make all things new, and to invite human beings to participate in that work as his apprentices. Without that focus, Christianity becomes just another religion—and who in the world needs that?

Despite differences of culture and theology, non-Catholics are increasingly recognizing in Ignatius Loyola one of the more helpful figures in the history of the church. Within that mysterious and wonderful thing called the body of Christ, there is much to learn from him. Maybe you would like to try doing the exercises some time—either during a forty-day retreat or following the Nineteenth Annotation—and discover it for yourself.

The experience might just bring that crazy busyness under control. And, what's more, it might help our church move with confidence into an uncertain future.

9

In Praise of Pietism

THIS WAS AN EDITORIAL *for* The Morning Star *in May 2004. I suppose it arose in part out of my experience of teaching in a seminary, where there is, traditionally at least, a separation of head and heart. I do think in recent years there has grown up a stronger tradition of holistic faith and theology, even in seminary, and the distinction I make here is not as pronounced as it was when the Enlightenment ruled academia. But the point was—and is still—worth making because the tendency to think in such binaries, in our faith and elsewhere, seems to be deeply rooted in human nature. This seemed to me also a good opportunity to introduce some students to John Wesley, whom evangelical Anglicans should know better than they generally do.*

Pietism, in my humble opinion, has had a bad rap.

I remember telling a friend once that I was sorry the hymn "Fairest Lord Jesus" was not known in British churches. He replied "Fairest Lord Jesus? That's just Pietist sentimentality!" (He was British.) So what's wrong with "Fairest Lord Jesus"? Well, it doesn't have a lot of doctrinal content, for one thing. The words could be summarized as saying, "Jesus is nicer than anything else in the world, e.g., meadows, woodlands, sunshine, moonlight, and the twinkling, starry host." Nothing in any of the creeds about the relative niceness of Jesus, as far as I recall. Nothing in Barth's *Church*

Dogmatics about that. And some of it is, frankly, nonsense: How can anyone compare Jesus to the sunlight or the moonlight, for example? Duh! Talk about comparing apples and oranges, or, rather, apples and—what can we say?—elephants, maybe?

Pietism has become a convenient swear word for a form of Christian spirituality which is individualistic, mindless, emotional, and lacking in theological backbone. In a word, mushy. Pietism, as it is popularly portrayed, thinks everything can be solved with a prayer and a verse of Scripture. Pietism says, "Praise the Lord!" on every possible occasion. Pietism seeks signs of God's guidance over the most trivial issues, like which socks to put on. (The good thing about that, of course, is someone at work may ask you why you are wearing odd socks, and then you have a chance to share the gospel.) Pietism talks freely about "the Lord" and the importance of loving Jesus. Pietists believe theology, or indeed, any serious thinking, can damage your spiritual health. They frequently don't go to movies, drink alcohol, get involved in politics, or indeed have anything to do with "the world."

Pietism, in other words, would not seem to jive well with a faith that is mature, thoughtful, and balanced. Pietism would certainly not appear to have a place in a community of serious theological learning. Indeed, the first Pietist students, meeting at the University of Leipzig in the seventeenth century, were told by the authorities, "Our mission is to make students more learned, not more pious," and their fellowship was dissolved.[1]

Yet Pietism had a more honorable and balanced beginning than all this might imply. The founder of the Pietist movement, Jakob Spener (1635–1705), was a German Lutheran. In the face of a church that was sterile and inward-looking, he began a movement for more serious Bible study, lay ministry, sacrificial discipleship, and love of enemies. The movement was given fresh impetus by Count Zinzendorf (1700–1760), who stressed "heart religion," "Christocentric piety, and reawakened zeal for a servant-missionary church informed by love."[2] Doesn't sound too awful, does it?

So can one be learned and pious, love God with heart and mind?

I would argue that not only can one be a scholar and pious, one darned well ought to be. Are there any models for such? One is John Wesley. While he was on board a ship bound for the USA in 1735, where he was going to be an Anglican missionary, a violent storm arose, and Wesley, like most people on board, feared for his life. A group of Moravian Christians, however, impressed him with their calmness, hymn-singing, and joyful prayer in the face of (apparently) imminent death.

---

1. Ferguson, *New Dictionary of Theology*, 516.
2. Brauer, *Westminster Dictionary of Church History*, 884.

"Moravians?" you ask. "Who are they?"

Part of the Pietist movement, that's who, directly influenced by Spener and Zinzendorf. As a result, Wesley realized his faith was lacking in a key dimension and began a pilgrimage that led him to a conversion experience through the friendship of Peter Bohler, another Moravian.

Wesley went on to become an amazing evangelist, trainer of lay leadership, and organizer, not to mention thorn in the flesh of the Church of England! What do you do with a priest like this? Where does he fit? He was also a significant self-taught theologian, who produced grammars of Latin, Greek, and Hebrew (among others), as well as editing a Greek New Testament and making his own translation of the Bible—all this while riding 4,000 miles a year on horseback and preaching a total of 40,000 sermons.

Wesley never lost that Pietist streak. After all, he wrote hymns such as the one that begins, "Thee will I love, my strength, my tower; thee will I love, my joy, my crown; thee will I love with all my power, in all thy works, and thee alone."[3] Classic Pietist stuff, eh? Love of Jesus, individual focus, not a lot of doctrinal content. But, you know what? Not many writers of Greek grammar also write what are basically love songs to Jesus, and not many hymn-writers could also write Greek grammars. Yet what a rich combination!

Can theology become arid and alienated from the life of the heart? Of course. Can Pietism be spineless and removed from the life of the mind? Of course. Someone has said (and I paraphrase), "Pietism alone would not be an adequate foundation for a church. On the other hand, without Pietism the church would lose its heart." John Wesley models how the two can live together comfortably in one person's skin, reinforce one another, and result in a spirituality of great and enduring power. "Pietist theologian" does not have to be an oxymoron.

---

3. *Common Praise*, #441.

10

"What are You Giving Up for Lent?"

A Meditation on Mortification

FROM TIME TO TIME *at our church, as in other churches, sermons follow a thematic series rather than the lectionary's set readings. In the fall of 2007, we did a series at St. John's called "The School of Jesus," intended as an introduction to the subject of discipleship. I forget who it was that first suggested "Mortification" as a suitable topic to include. It's possible it was me, and that I meant it as a half-joke. But then I suggested that it would be a good challenge for someone to try and make what sounds like a forbidding and gloomy topic something that would make sense and give life. Strangely enough, none of the other preachers wanted to claim it, so you can guess what happened. I hope I succeeded.*

If I say the word "mortification," what comes to your mind? Nothing very cheerful, I'm guessing. We say, "I was mortified," when we feel we might die of embarrassment. A mortician's job sounds suspiciously as though it might have something to do with mortification. And then there's all that stuff about monks and self-flagellation in Dan Brown's *The Da Vinci Code*: mortification again.

So, is there anything Christian about such a concept? Certainly the apostle Paul seems to have thought so: "Put to death, therefore, whatever belongs to your earthly nature," he urges in Colossians 3:5. Or, as the King James Version put it: "Mortify therefore your members which are upon the earth." That's the origin of this ugly term, "mortification." You may say, But it sounds so negative! Surely Christianity is a religion about life? Jesus came to bring us "life in all its fullness," not "death in all its emptiness"!

Of course, this is Paul. And many would ask, "Do we need to worry what Paul thought? He was just a crabby, misogynistic old bachelor . . . We are followers of Jesus, not of Paul."

But there is more of Jesus than we like to admit in the teaching of Paul. (I think I began to realize this when someone pointed out that the Epistle to the Romans is fundamentally a commentary on the parable of the runaway son and his older brother.) Paul was not particularly trying to be original in his teaching. Like us, he was trying to come to terms with who Jesus was and what he taught. He too was a follower of Jesus.

So could this negative kind of talk about "putting to death" have come from Paul's understanding of Jesus? Examples are not hard to find. "Cut off your hand, pluck out your eye!" (Matt 5:30) says Jesus. "Take up your cross! Deny yourself!" (Luke 9:23). So this really does originate with Jesus. Paul is not turning Jesus' message of sweetness and light into a miserable anti-life diatribe.

Let me say first: the idea of "mortifying" things is not just a weird religious idea. Everybody has experienced this kind of putting to death. Parents who get up in the night to feed the baby put to death their desire for a good night's sleep. People who give up smoking put to death their addiction to tobacco. People who work out put to death their preference for sitting in front of the TV. Now, we know why those people do these things. But why does Paul say disciples of Jesus should put things to death?

The blunt answer is: because there is stuff in our lives which will kill us unless we kill it first. We like to say "There is good in everyone"—and that is true. But—although it's not very popular to say it—there is also evil in everyone, and that's harder to swallow. Russian novelist Aleksandr Solzhenitsyn puts it this way:

> The line separating good and evil passes . . . through every human heart. . . . Even within hearts overwhelmed by evil, one small bridgehead of good is retained; and even in the best of all hearts, there remains a small corner of evil.[1]

But isn't this a very negative thing in Christianity, something we should have moved beyond by this time? Well, a good principle for understanding the Bible is to approach the difficult stuff from the point-of-view of the stuff that is clearer. So let's start with what we know.

---

1. Solzhenitsyn, *Gulag Archipelago Two*, 615–16.

The first and most important thing is this: Jesus teaches us that God loves us; three little words, but absolutely amazing—enough to change your life, enough to change the world.

And what does God's love mean? Simply, that God wants the absolute best for us. In particular, it means that God wants to shape us into the people God made us to be, not just as individuals but as a community. If you like, God wants to restore the image of God in us.

That's why God calls us to follow Jesus. By following Jesus we become the people God created us to be. God's purpose is entirely positive. God's ultimate goal is that the universe should be filled with joy.

Here is where things are not quite so straightforward, however. Sometimes the best route from A to B is not a straight line. Sometimes it means going backwards in order to go forwards.

On the one hand, God wants to nurture the good in us, but on the other hand, in order to do that, God needs to deal with what's wrong in us—because in all of us there are weeds which threaten to overwhelm the good growth God is nurturing in us.

So how do we kill bad things in our lives? Sometimes it can be done gradually, but sometimes it has to be done quickly. In C. S. Lewis's *The Great Divorce*, for example, there is a man who arrives at the edge of heaven with a red lizard on his shoulder. The man wants to stay but the lizard doesn't. An angel offers to kill the lizard if the man wants. The man isn't sure: he thinks the angel would end up killing him and not just the lizard. The angel says no: the man would be hurt but he wouldn't die. Only the lizard would die.

Eventually the man agrees. The angel reaches out and breaks the back of the lizard. But then a strange thing happens: the man turns into a new man—big, beautiful, bright, and shining, a little like the angel—but even stranger, the lizard turns into a great stallion. Then the man mounts the stallion and they ride off into deep heaven.[2]

Lewis, it seems, would agree that there are some things that threaten us which can be dealt with once and for all. His story also makes the point very nicely that the reason we put things to death is so new life can come.

On the other hand, there are many things that can be put to death only gradually—by starvation, if you like. It takes time. It takes the strength and the courage of the Holy Spirit to say "No" every day. And it means cutting myself off from the things that feed my temptation.

The story is told of a little boy whose father had told him not to go in the swimming pool. Later that day, his father found him by the pool with

---

2. Lewis, *Great Divorce*, 106–12.

his swimsuit in his hand. "Weren't you told you couldn't go swimming?" asked his father.

"I'm not going swimming," said the boy.

"Then why have you got your swimsuit?"

"Oh, that's in case I get tempted."

If you know you shouldn't go in the pool, don't go near the pool . . . and certainly don't take your swimsuit.

All of us have these things in our lives that threaten the new life God is trying to grow in us. I'm sure you can think of examples from your own life, but here are a few that come to my mind immediately:

- Many of us worry. Indeed, we have lists of things to worry about. Mortification can mean saying "No" to those worries: putting ourselves in the presence of God for a few minutes (what some people call "the sacred pause") and trying to see things from God's point of view.
- Many churches sell Fair Trade coffee. They could get cheaper coffee elsewhere, of course. But they mortify their desire to save a few dollars, and help bring life to the coffee producers.
- At the end of a Sunday morning service, our instinct is to talk to our friends. But, of course, when there are visitors, that natural instinct has to be put to death, and we try to cultivate something which does not come quite so naturally, at least for us introverts—talking to new people.

A story about our son Ben—a jazz trumpeter—helps me get my head around this whole thing. When he was in his teens, after some years of learning trumpet, he got a new teacher who happened to be one of the top trumpet players in Canada. And Mr. Oades said, "You're doing it all wrong. If you want to develop in your playing, you're going to have to start over, and relearn your embouchure."

Did Ben do it? He could have said, "No way. I've spent years playing this way, and I feel comfortable with it. Don't cramp my style." But he didn't. He obeyed the teacher, turned his back on the way he'd been playing before, and, as a result, he was able to move ahead in his playing, way beyond where he would have got to any other means.

Sometimes it is the same for students of Jesus. Yes, there are positive things Jesus asks us to do—but sometimes he asks us to do something that seems negative, to turn our backs on things we love, things that seem like death to give up.

But in fact, it's a death that leads to life. Good Friday is the only way to Easter.

11

Getting Good and Angry

IN THE LATE 1970S, *we were still in our first home in Toronto and, for complicated reasons, I took myself to see a counselor. One of the things we talked about during those sessions was anger, which had not been an acceptable emotion in my upbringing. What follows is among the many helpful things I learned from this man.*

One indication of his influence is that the ideas which follow have stuck with me since then. The first version of this article was published in the 1980s in The New Edinburgh News, *our local newspaper in Ottawa, as part of a regular column that I was contributing on the subject of words. Then in March 2002 I reworked it as an editorial for* The Morning Star. *And just last week, strangely enough, I sent it to my teenage granddaughter, who is getting interested in words. That's forty years.*

Sometimes the Greek language fills in the blanks when we find ourselves speechless. It is Greek that has provided us with such indispensable daily terms as technology, television, and kinetic energy. But that's a case of us borrowing their words to describe our reality. Sometimes, however, their perception of reality was rather finer than ours, and they have more words than we really know what to do with. C. S. Lewis was one of the first I am aware of to help us poor Anglophones enjoy the sophistication, not just of

Greek vocabulary (though that's always useful for impressing friends), but of the understanding of life which their vocabulary portrayed.

My classical education hardly went beyond "amo, amas, I love a lass, and she's of the feminine gender." But with the help of Lewis's *The Four Loves*, the Greek language opened some windows on life which I suppose I knew were there, but which were somehow always steamed up so that the world outside was blurred. Although the book was written in the 1950s, and although some of the arcane learning and dry academic wit date the book a little, it still brings a miraculous clarity into that confused morass we call "love."

Lewis points out that the ancient Greeks divided the labor done in English by a single over-worked word—love—between four distinct words, each with its own separate meaning.

There was *storge* (pronounced store-gay)—family affection; *philia*—friendship (hence Philadelphia, city of brotherly love); *eros*—the desire to possess (not only sexually); and *agape* (aga-pay)—self-sacrificing love for the unlovely, a usage which came into being at the beginning of the Christian era.

"I love you" has always been one of the most potent yet confusing phrases in the English language. "Love is love," people say. Well, not actually. At least we can now respond (if we have the presence of mind), "Do you mean you think of me as your mother, you enjoy playing golf with me, you want to go to bed with me, or you'll sell your shirt to help me, ugly though I am?" It is as well to be clear about these things. Although the context may not always allow such a leisurely and thoughtful response.

There is a second area where the Greeks subdivided what we in our naivety usually treat as a single topic: anger. Even more than love, we normally treat anger as if it were a single thing—explosive, unpredictable, often violent. As a result, most of us have very ambivalent feelings about anger. On the one hand, the inhibited fifties taught those of us who grew up then that anger was nasty, dangerous and certainly not to be expressed in civilized society. Then, when the sixties hit, the emotional dam was unstopped, and it was OK to feel anything at all: we "let it all hang out" (a phrase that was invented to describe this new discovery). So on the one hand, most of us live with a feeling that expressing anger is somehow healthy and necessary. On the other hand, we have inherited the knowledge that it can also destroy, not only things, but people.

A little Greek sheds a lot of light. This I picked up from a psychiatrist a long time ago, and never forgot:

First, the Greeks talked about *orge* (or-gay). That is the basic, raw emotion. You stub your toe, or the baby won't stop crying, or the car won't start on the very morning you overslept, and you get that rising tide of hot emotion, beginning somewhere around your stomach—*orge* in full flood. For the Greeks, this was morally neutral. You can't help it, after all. There is something lousy going on which has caused the anger. Often we perceive that an injustice is being done, usually towards ourselves, but not always— "That's just not fair!"—and it makes us mad.

The reason we do not normally think of anger as neutral is that in practice it often gets confused with the second kind: *thumos*. *Thumos* is an angry act. You stub your toe, so you kick the rock that did it—and hurt the other foot too. The baby won't sleep, so you shout at it and it cries all the more. The car won't start, so you take it out on people at the office when you finally get there forty-five minutes late. *Thumos* is the reaction to *orge*. *Orge* is something you feel; *thumos* is something you do. *Orge* is not something you decide; *thumos* involves a decision of the will.

Often our dis-ease with anger arises because we are so used to there being no distinction between the first two angers. I feel angry, therefore I lash out. But the Greeks were a bit more subtle in their psychological understanding. We may feel angry—even ten times a day—but on each occasion, we can choose what to do about it. Confusing the two means we are tempted to dismiss all anger as bad and destructive; or alternatively, to think that every time we get mad the only way out is physical or verbal violence.

Watching a World Vision special about world hunger highlights some of the reality the Greeks perceived. I suspect everyone who watches those things feels anger in among the other emotions. The number of people who phone in to offer a donation tells you that most people find a constructive way to channel that anger. They see injustice, they feel *orge*, and they choose to do one of the few things they can do to help right the wrong: they give their money.

Now, I don't know, but it is at least conceivable that people watching those shows express their *orge* in different ways. They may smash the TV. Or write to the TV channel about emotional blackmail. They may kick the cat, or get drunk, or a hundred other possibilities. Those responses are *thumos*: an angry response to the feeling of *orge*.

The moral choice involved in anger came home to me one day when our first child was very small—maybe two years old. I came home one day to find his willful perversity had reduced my wife to helpless tears. I was angry—and put my fist straight through the wall. A couple minutes later, while nursing my fist and wondering how much it would cost to repair the wall, I thought about what had happened. I realized with awe that in the split second between feeling anger and hitting the wall, I had made a choice—a choice not to hit the person I perceived to be responsible for an injustice, but to take it out on the wall instead. The feeling and the action were actually separate things. I wasn't especially proud of my response—but it could have been a lot worse. *Orge* doesn't force you to do anything, but it does present you with a choice.

The third kind of anger is *perorgismos*—just as nasty as the name sounds. This is anger that is not dealt with appropriately, and which festers like an untreated wound. *Perorgismos* is a fire that smolders, maybe for years, without being either doused or fanned into flame. We fondle the memory of the wrong done—usually to us—until it becomes a part of us we do not want to lose, and maybe could not even if we wanted to. I recently came across a story about a husband and wife who had communicated only by means of notes for twenty years. *Perorgismos*. For the Greeks, this was unnecessary and morally immature. Better a good dose of *thumos* and get it over with.

Finally there is *ekthra*. *Ekthra* is anger which has become a way of life. *Ekthra* is the blood feud, the tribal warfare. *Ekthra* is the Capulets and the Montagues in ancient Verona, Protestants and Catholics in Northern Ireland during the Troubles. There is a sense in *ekthra* of choosing this person as my enemy, and of something perversely enjoyable in being committed to their undoing.

When we say, "I hate her," usually we mean no more than "I'm really angry at her." But *ekthra* is true hatred: deliberately setting oneself to destroy another. The British TV series *Mapp and Lucia* (now available on YouTube) pictured it exquisitely, as two ageing upper-class Englishwomen tried to destroy one another with infinite refinement and delicate ruthlessness. True hatred. Deliciously funny to watch, not so great to live with.

So when the boss calls you in tomorrow morning, slams his fist on the desk, and announces, "I am angry," why not ask, "Yes, sir, but what exactly do you mean by angry?" On second thought, maybe not. His Greek may not be as good as yours.

C

Worldly Wisdom

THE CHURCH EXISTS IN two modes: gathered and scattered. The distinction is obvious, I suppose. To my mind, the two are equally important. The classroom and the placement, the study and the practicum, are both essential to healthy learning. Yet most of the time "church" is associated with the gathered mode, for the obvious reason that you can't see or easily identify the church in its scattered mode. You know where the church is on Sunday, but on Monday it has mysteriously vanished.

For obvious reasons, seminaries tend to focus on training leaders for Sunday mornings. Which means, in turn, that ordained ministers tend to treat Sunday as the most important day of the week—and, for them, it may well be. But what about the rest of the week? These articles and sermons address what Paul Stevens called *The Other Six Days*.[1]

---

1. Stevens, *Other Six Days*.

12

Vacuum Cleaner Church

WHEN I DIRECTED THE Institute of Evangelism at Wycliffe College, we put out a monthly newsletter called "Good Idea!" (The exclamation mark, which I inherited from the previous editor, was important.) The vision statement of the Institute was "Every church an evangelizing community," so every article addressed some aspect of the church's life and mission. Our mailing list consisted of ministers and other leaders in churches across Canada, mainly but by no means exclusively Anglican. ("Good Idea!" still exists and thrives, and you can join the list via the Institute's website.)

A variety of authors contributed, and occasionally I would take a turn—especially if I had a bee in my bonnet. This particular bee had been buzzing for a long time, probably decades, so it was time to let it go free. Unfortunately, the bee has been provoked to buzz back rather frequently since then, which is why the article is reprinted here. This version was published in February 2014.

Have you heard the term "vacuum cleaner church?" Whether you've heard it or not, you've probably experienced it. "Oh, can you help out with this committee? Can you do a reading this Sunday? Why don't you join this small group?" It goes on and on. I remember a friend joking that there was only one night a week when she was at home, and her husband was worried that she'd give that one up to being at the church too. It wasn't a particularly funny joke.

The trouble is that it is all too easy to measure people's spiritual maturity by the amount of time they spend in the four walls of the church building, or in church-related activities. They're the people we value most, the people we trust with yet more responsibilities, and the people we reward.

WHAT IS THE CHURCH?

What is wrong with this picture? It assumes a very distorted understanding of the church. What is church? Church consists of those who have responded to God's call to repent and believe through faith and baptism. And what does repent and believe mean? Jesus connects it with his announcement of "the kingdom" (Mark 1:15). So we could paraphrase Jesus' words about the arrival of the kingdom this way: "Now I'm here, God's plan to restore and renew the world is reaching its climax: drop whatever you're doing and come join me. Stop wasting your lives and get with God's program!"

If this is the heart of church, then how does it operate? Some have suggested that church exists in two modes, the gathered mode (when we come together for worship and teaching) and the scattered mode (the rest of the week, when we live our lives in the places God has called us—home, work, or leisure). Church is an apprenticeship in the ways of the kingdom, a co-op program with a (relatively small) classroom component, and an on-the-job component (most of the time).

The trouble is, church leaders usually value the gathered mode more than the scattered mode. It's natural enough, since—traditionally anyway—the focus of seminary training has been how to lead the church in gathered mode with excellence. But Lesslie Newbigin warned, over a quarter of a century ago, that this is not enough:

> It seems clear that ministerial training as currently conceived is still far too much training for pastoral care of the existing congregation, and far too little oriented towards the missionary calling to claim the whole of public life for Christ and his kingdom.[1]

Did you notice the word "still" in there? He was looking back—as long ago as 1977!—and seeing that even then this was a long-standing problem. So has it changed since then?

---

1. Newbigin, *Gospel in a Pluralist Society*, 230–31.

THE NEED FOR MISSIONAL LEADERSHIP

In recent years, some seminaries have begun to reorient their teaching and training to take on a missional dimension: that is, like the church in general, we have realized that the purpose of the church is to work with God in God's mission to renew and restore the cosmos. The church is not there to supply services to religious consumers, or to meet people's spiritual needs, or to provide a spiritual dimension to society's life. We are a community of Jesus Christ's apprentices, working with him towards the transformation of the world for the glory of God. This is the key to understanding Scripture. This helps us know who we are meant to be in a post-Christendom world.

But I'm not sure this awareness has percolated through into the life of the average local church. Our instinct is still to suck people into innumerable activities—all of them worthwhile, of course—within the church community (and all too often in the church building), instead of seeing church events as equipping Christians for their missionary work in the world.

John Stott warned us of this danger almost forty years ago:

> A convert to Jesus Christ lives in the world as well as in the church, and has responsibilities to the world as well as to the church. I think it is the tendency of churches to "ecclesiasticize" their members which has made so many modern Christians understandably wary . . . Conversion must not take the convert out of the world but rather send him back into it, the same person in the same world, and yet a new person with new convictions and new standards. If Jesus' first command was "Come," his second was "Go"—that is, we are to go back into the world out of which we have come, and go back as Christ's ambassadors.[2]

Rather than honoring those who spend all their time in church, perhaps we should worry about them. How will they ever mature as apprentices of Jesus that way? How will they have time to fulfill their mission in the world? Of course, some people are required—and gifted—to maintain existing church structures. After all, we do need those structures to equip and sustain us for mission. But my hunch is that not as many people are needed, and not as often.

Maybe some of those who are in gathered mode too much of the time need to be pushed out of the nest so they can learn to fly—for their own good and the good of the mission. The opposite is also worth considering. We sometimes worry about those who only show up on Sundays, and resist serving on church committees. We even question their commitment: are

---

2. Stott, *Christian Mission in the Modern World*, 121.

they really growing in their discipleship? But it may be that, if we scratched the surface of those people's lives, we would find they are too involved with loving their neighbors to serve on yet another church committee.

SENDING OUT, NOT SUCKING IN

I had a friend once who started literally dozens of Bible study groups in workplaces across his city. Over the years, they saw about a hundred people come to Christian faith through their witness. My friend's church—a Baptist church—said, "Look, we would love to have you as one of our elders, but this work you are doing across the city is your mission, and putting you on a church committee would just be a waste of your gifts. So we will pray for you and support you in any way we can." A truly missional response. After some years, my friend moved to a job on the other side of the country. So the man who had acted as Vice-President of the group was asked to take over the leadership. His response? "I would love to do that, but I'm much too busy in my church. Thanks, but no thanks." Not surprisingly, the ministry declined in size and effectiveness.

Jesus said we are the salt of the earth. Good Christian leaders will ensure that the salt gets sprinkled liberally where it is most needed, and beware the piles that accumulate on the side of the plate. Or, to change the image: Christians are rather like manure: spread thinly, they do a great job. But gather too many of them together for too long, and they begin to smell pretty bad.

13

Serving God on the Inside and on the Outside

It is always good to acknowledge sources, so I admit I first heard this way of thinking about Elijah and Obadiah in the 1970s, in a sermon by Roy Clements, at that time pastor of Eden Baptist Church in Cambridge, UK. But I am solely responsible for the spin I have put on it, for better or for worse.

I first wrote this article in October 1996, but the question of Christians' relationship to the secular world is a perennial one. Reinhold Niebuhr famously traced five ways the relationship has been worked out in church history in his 1950 classic, Christ and Culture. *My approach here addresses two of his models, though my conclusion is not his. I use the example of politics here, because the article was first inspired by criticism of Christian politicians in the church media, but the application is much wider than that. See what you think.*

Are Christians in politics inevitably involved in compromise? The question is not a new one. It goes back at least as far as the time of Ahab, king of Israel. Here a newly discovered correspondence from the Dead Sea Scrolls sheds light on the question. (With apologies to 1 Kings 17 and 18.)

Dear Obadiah:

I knew from the moment you got appointed to Ahab's court that there'd be trouble. How can you expect to serve God and Ahab? It just can't be done.

Now I read in *Israel Today* that he's married this pagan woman, Jezebel, who wants to root out all traces of the old faith. And is it true that she's planning to murder all known prophets of Yahweh?

Seems to me, Obadiah, that your being there hasn't made the slightest bit of difference. If anything, the royal court is getting worse daily, and you're getting dragged down with it.

Yahweh's true people have always been outsiders. Remember how Moses left the corrupt court of Pharaoh? Think about it, Obadiah. Get out of there while you've got the chance. Come and join us in the hills. The fellowship is wonderful. "No compromise": that's our motto. How about it?

Your brother,
Elijah

Dear Elijah:

Thank you for your invitation. For the time being, I think the Lord is calling me to stay here. You may be right that the time will come when I should leave. But I don't think it's yet.

You are right that Jezebel is planning to legalize the slaughter of the prophets. However, I was able to persuade her to limit it to prophets within the city of Jerusalem itself. That's something. Some of them will be able to escape while she's getting organized. But she is a very determined woman, Elijah, and Ahab is fickle as water.

By the way, I seem to remember Moses stayed in the court of Pharaoh as long as he could. And you might recall that Joseph even became Pharaoh's Prime Minister, and served Yahweh's people well from the inside.

Your old friend,
Obadiah

Dear Obadiah:

Your letter arrived this morning, and I wanted to write back straight away because its tone worried me. Do I detect a hidden ambition, Obadiah? Could it be that what you are really seeking is not Yahweh's glory but simply to become Ahab's prime minister?

SERVING GOD ON THE INSIDE AND ON THE OUTSIDE

You should know how subtly temptations creep up on us: "I'm sure I can serve the Lord better if I accept this high office. Too bad about the salary and the prestige, but I guess I can put up with it." Don't kid yourself, friend. Riches and status make God's people spiritually blind.

What is worse, I hope you realize that the blood of those prophets will be upon your head. You might as well have signed the death warrant yourself for those within the city. You have betrayed Yahweh and his people by this sickening compromise.

Get out, Obadiah, before judgment descends on Ahab, and you catch it too. You may already have left it too late.

Elijah

Dear Elijah:

It's all very well for you to descend from your ivory tower every six months and march with placards outside the palace walls. Denouncing Ahab and Jezebel doesn't change a thing. That's just too easy. Frankly, your prophetic style is cheap.

I don't want to boast, Elijah, but it's people like me who face these pagans with the reality of Yahwism day to day who really make a difference. And it's not easy, let me tell you, living among them every day. But that's where the rubber of faith hits the road of real life. You should try it some time. Then you might not be so quick with your criticisms.

As for compromise, frankly, it saves lives. Every prophet outside the city is safe—thanks to me, I am tempted to say. Your dogmatism, on the other hand, only serves to make the opposition more determined.

Obadiah

Obadiah:

You've clearly lost your sense of direction. We are meant to be a pure Yahwist nation, and our job is to call the people back to their roots. Seems to me you're just getting swept up into everything that's going on: this woman with her feminist power-trips and her goddesses. Makes me sick. But you seem able to stomach it all right.

Being in these godforsaken places day in and day out is cutting down the spiritual sensitivity you used to have. Frankly, I fear for the state of your soul.

I am planning to come and confront the court with some black-and-white issues—soon.

Praying for you,
Elijah

Elijah:

It's really no use at all going on about our Israelite origins. Face it, we live in a post-Yahwist society. Nobody takes Yahweh seriously anymore, nobody listens to the Torah. Baalism is all the rage.

But what you don't seem to realize is that their majesties actually take me seriously. Just the other day, the king told me how much he appreciated my advice, and asked if I would pray for him. The trouble with your approach is that it's simply too easy for everyone to laugh at you and dismiss you as an eccentric.

What's more, I utterly fail to see what you can possibly achieve by this confronting of Ahab and the prophets of Baal. You could totally undermine the slow, steady witness of people like me—and there are a number of us. I hope you know what you're doing.

Frustratedly,
Obadiah

My dear Obadiah:

I sensed that you were praying yesterday. Thank you. I have done my part and I feel utterly drained. Now it is over to you. Ahab will not speak to me. Clearly Yahweh has you there for an hour such as this.

I hear too that you were able to save a hundred of Yahweh's prophets from that woman last month. Only you could have done that. Why did you not tell me? But I think I know why.

Forgive me my harsh criticisms of earlier letters. You know how impetuous and dogmatic I can get.

Your covenant brother,
Elijah

Brother Elijah:

Thank you for that awesome demonstration on the hill yesterday. Generations to come will call that your finest hour. Your courage humbles me. Yahweh has not forsaken us after all.

Ahab has been asking me questions about the faith ever since. Pray that he will return to the Lord with all his heart.

Your brother,
Obadiah

14

The Vocation of a Garbage Collector

IN THE FALL OF 2010, the theme of Thursday faculty sermons in chapel was *Vocation*. This is a topic frequently and earnestly discussed in seminaries—"Am I called to ordination?" "Do I have a vocation to the priesthood?" "How do I discern my vocation?" and so on. As a so-called layperson involved in so-called nonordained ministry most of my so-called adult life, and having been deeply affected by a Reformed view of life, I have what seems to some a rather unconventional view of this topic.

If a Christian in a Toronto suburb collects garbage for a living, is that her vocation? If you think yes, put your hand up. If no, put your hand up. If you think there is a catch but you're not sure what it is, put your hand up. If you wish people wouldn't ask difficult questions first thing in the morning . . . yes, I thought so.

We'll come back to that question in a moment. I will only say for now: Yes, it is a trick question. But you knew that already.

I want to begin by looking at what the New Testament, specifically Paul, says about calling and vocation. Evangelicals look to the Bible for authoritative teaching to shape our doctrine and our ministry: right? And yet at the same time we want to honor tradition and the way Christians have read these same Scriptures before. So what happens when what Scripture teaches is different from what we have traditionally been told? I will leave it to you to wrestle with that one. I think Jesus is pretty clear on the issue! So, on this specific issue, suffice it to say, the New Testament is very clear about what vocation and calling are (the terms are interchangeable), and it is equally clear that it is a long way from the way we use the terms these days.

Here are some examples. After I say, "What is your vocation? Your vocation is X," I invite you to respond, "My vocation is X." OK?

1. 1 Corinthians 1:9: "God is faithful, by him you were called into the fellowship of his Son."
   What is your vocation? Your vocation is to be in fellowship with Jesus Christ.
   My vocation is to be in fellowship with Jesus Christ.

2. 1 Corinthians 7:15: It is to peace that God has called you.
   What is your vocation? Your vocation is to participate in the *shalom* of God.
   My vocation is to participate in the shalom *of God.*

3. Galatians 1:6: "I am astonished that you are so quickly deserting the one who called you in the grace of Christ.
   What is your vocation? Your vocation is to experience the grace of Christ.
   My vocation is to experience the grace of Christ.

4. Galatians 5:13: You were called to freedom!
   What is your vocation? Your vocation is to be free in Christ.
   My vocation is to be free in Christ.

5. Ephesians 1:18: "that you may know the hope to which he has called you."
   What is your vocation? Your vocation is to have hope in Christ.
   My vocation is to have hope in Christ.

6. 1 Thessalonians 2:12: "Lead a life worthy of God who calls you into his own kingdom and glory."
   What is your vocation? Your vocation is to participate in God's kingdom and glory.
   My vocation is to participate in God's kingdom and glory.

Do you get it? St. Paul consistently uses the term "vocation" to refer to our calling to be Christians. There is no higher vocation. This is the highest calling any human being could ever have. There is none greater—at least, according to the New Testament. This is what human beings were made for. This is why Christ died. This is why the Holy Spirit was given. So that we might know our vocation: to be children of God, to be eternally loved by the Triune God.

I know, I know, we want to ask, "That's all very nice, but I need to know how God wants me to live my life. Am I called to marry or to be single? Am I called to be ordained or lay? Am I called to be an architect, a homemaker, a police officer, a pastor or (God forbid) a seminary professor? That's the really important question."

But it's not the really important question. That's a secondary question. People in monastic orders who are called to ordination refer to a calling within a calling: called first to be a monk or a nun, and then secondarily within that bigger calling to be in ordained ministry.

I want to suggest that whatever a Christian does with his or her life is always like that: it's a calling within a calling. The New Testament never uses the words "vocation" or "calling" to describe what you should do with your life. Never.[1] So it is unbiblical to do so! It would be more biblical not to call that second calling a calling at all, but something else—a leading, perhaps (since the shepherd leads his flock). Assuming we're not going to adopt a biblical way of thinking in this respect any time soon (and I think that's pretty safe to assume), then at least let's distinguish between Calling with a capital C and calling with a small c—and remember, for God's sake, which is which.

This confusion over vocation is the reason I chose what might seem at first to be an irrelevant reading. The chapter is not about vocation. That much is immediately obvious. But what is revealing here is what Paul simply takes for granted about vocation, and about how we are to spend our lives. You'll notice he uses the word "call" or "calling" eight times in these eight verses:

> Let each of you lead the life that the Lord has assigned, [in] which God called you. This is my rule in all the churches. Was anyone at the time of his call already circumcised? Let him not seek to remove the marks of circumcision. Was anyone at the time of his call uncircumcised? Let him not seek circumcision. Circumcision is nothing, and uncircumcision is nothing; but obeying the commandments of God is everything. Let each of

---

1. Some have queried whether Paul's description of himself as "called to be an apostle of Jesus Christ" does not seem to suggest at least one exception. However, the Greek phrase is simply "*paulos kletos apostolos iesou*"—Paul called apostle of Jesus Christ—where "called" is an adjective describing "apostle," i.e., "a called (that is, a Christian) apostle." The words "to be" are a translator's addition.

you remain in the condition in which you were called. Were you a slave when called? Do not be concerned about it. Even if you can gain your freedom, make use of your present condition now more than ever. For whoever was called in the Lord as a slave is a freed person belonging to the Lord, just as whoever was free when called is a slave of Christ. You were bought with a price; do not become slaves of human masters. In whatever condition you were called, brothers and sisters, there remain with God (1 Cor 7:17–24).

His basic contention is this: whatever state you were in when you were called, stay there. If you were married, or circumcised, or a slave—stay that way. Your calling in Christ is not first and foremost a sign that you should change anything externally. It does mean change, and big changes too—in three dimensions, as it were. First, it means a change in relationship: whatever your situation, you are now there "with God" (24), and that makes all the difference in the world. Then it is a change in your status: "For whoever was called in the Lord as a slave is a freed person belonging to the Lord, just as whoever was free when called is a slave of Christ." Whoever you are, now you belong to Christ, whose service is perfect freedom (22). And, third, there is a change in your behavior, now that "obeying the commandments of God is everything" (19). Your new job is to love God and love your neighbor. So there are huge changes which flow out of your calling—in your relationships ("with God"), in your status ("belonging to Christ"), and in your behavior ("obeying . . . God")—but they are the fruit of your calling, not themselves the calling.

So how should I spend my life, supposing I have a choice (and let's remember that most people in the history of the world have had few choices)? There are two clues as to how Paul views the question in this chapter. Number one, he says: go with your gifts. This is not in our passage, but just before. In verse 7, he is speaking of marriage, and he says, "each has a particular gift from God, one having one kind and another a different kind." Some traditions speak of marriage as a vocation, a calling: Paul speaks of it as something for which you have a gift, a supernatural endowment (the word is *charism*, from which we get the term charismatic gifts). That's one way you decide how to serve God: what gifts (*charisms*) has God given you? Being married, being single, pastoring, teaching, designing stuff, looking after children, taking care of the environment, artistic creation: these are all gifts God has implanted in our DNA—not really callings or vocations, except in that small-c way.

But, number two, Paul also says: take what opportunities you may have. In verse 21, he says to slaves: "Even if you can gain your freedom, make use of your present condition now more than ever." It's more literally, "If you can become free, rather use it." Whether he's saying "make the most of being a slave," or "make the most of your freedom," scholars are not sure, but he's certainly saying, "Be pragmatic." How do you decide how to spend your life? One way is to watch what opportunities come along and to take them. (As I look back on my own life, that explains a number of choices I felt "led" to make.) Will you go wrong? Not if you're seeking to be a servant of Christ—that is, to fulfill or to live out your calling, your vocation. As Augustine said, "Love God and do what you like."[2]

How then do I know how I should spend my life? Paul would seem to be saying, "Ask, what are my gifts? And what are my opportunities? Don't look for a Large-C vocation: you've already got that."

So what about our Christian garbage collector? Is that work her vocation? You can answer that yourselves. Answer number one: no, her vocation is to be a child of God and a disciple of Jesus Christ, and to serve with great dignity and dedication and joy. But in that secondary sense, of a calling (small c) within a Calling (large C), yes, it is her vocation to represent Jesus Christ and his kingdom in her world, by being the very best garbage collector she can be—just as you and I, whether theology student, professor, staff member, accountant, secretary, maintenance staff, cleaner, priest or lay, represent him in our worlds.

What is your vocation? Your vocation is to be known and loved by Christ, and to make him known in your world. Everything else is secondary. This is why the Greek for church is *ekklesia*: it's made up exclusively of those who are called. Say it to yourself frequently though the day, and when you wake up in the night. Say it to one another, say it to me, say it to your professors, say it to your pastor. There is no greater reality, no greater vocation, than to be a child of God, a disciple of Jesus Christ, and the dwelling place of the Holy Spirit. Thanks be to God for his amazing calling to us.

---

2. Augustine, "Homily VII."

15

Discipleship on the Front Lines

We all pontificate about things of which we have no experience. Life after death is the universal example. But we also speak about the lives of politicians, or drug dependence, or what it would mean to live on other planets, as if we knew what we are talking about. Sometimes people challenge us, but much of the time we get away with it.

Having to preach on the topic of "Discipleship in Everyday Life" at St. John's in November 2017 brought this home to me. I know something of the lives of many in the congregation, not least what work they do, and how seriously they take their call to discipleship. So I decided that, while I could frame this topic, I needed to let them speak about the areas where they spend their days, and where I have never been. You will quickly come to see why I love this community. You will also see why this chapter follows the previous one.

Have you ever considered which jobs God likes best? What kind of work God wants his people to do? Which are the most spiritual?

Many of us have in our minds a hierarchy we would never say out loud about how God likes people to spend their time. God likes people to do spiritual things in spiritual places with spiritual people. Right?

So people like archbishops, bishops, clergy, missionaries, and theological educators (I had to get that in) are clearly high in God's approval ratings.

Doctors and nurses are pretty high on the list too, then teachers, perhaps social workers (depending on their politics), and then everybody else, and right at the bottom, of course, politicians. And those at the top of the list we consider spiritual, and those in the bottom half are secular. Right? Like this:[1]

> Spiritual	• Archbishops
	• Bishops
	• Pastors
	• Missionaries
	• Theological educators
> Secular	• Doctors
	• Nurses
	• Teachers
	• Social workers
	• Everyone else
	• Politicians

But what if that's not right? What if the line between spiritual and secular isn't that way at all? What if it isn't a horizontal line at all, but a vertical line? The line would then go right through the middle of each job on the list, from the archbishop to the politician. Like this:

> Spiritual	• Arch	bishops	> Secular
	• Bish	ops	
	• Past	ors	
	• Miss	ionaries	
	• Theo	logical educators	
	• Doct	ors	
	• Nurs	es	
	• Teac	hers	
	• Soci	al workers	
	• Ever	yone else	
	• Poli	ticians	

People doing a job in the top half of that list will tell you there are ways of doing those jobs that bring glory to God, and ways that very definitely don't. And there are people doing jobs in the lower half of the list who very

---

1. These two diagrams are adapted from Wolters, *Creation Regained*, 68.

clearly do those jobs to the glory of God (including politicians!) as well as some who don't.

So what makes a job outside church spiritual? What does it mean to do a nonreligious job to the glory of God? This is where discipleship fits in. Being an apprentice to Jesus doesn't just happen in church or in personal relationships. For forty hours a week (or however many it may be) our apprenticeship to Jesus takes place in the workplace. So what exactly does that look like?

Since I was twenty-six, I've worked in church-related jobs, so I can't really pontificate on the subject. So this week I asked a number of folk in the congregation who are in nonreligious jobs (which is not the same as nonspiritual) how this works for them. Let me share some of the answers with you.

1. THEIR WORKPLACE IS WHERE JESUS TEACHES THEM THE WAYS OF THE KINGDOM

"One recent insight which cracked my (I was going to say thick skull, but is actually my) hard heart, I guess, is how Jesus responded to the rich young ruler asking about how to live: 'Jesus looked at him and loved him.' I think he is helping me to look at people and remember how he loved people and that is what he wants us to do." —Margaret, physiotherapist

There's Margaret taking a specific story about Jesus, and thinking how his example might shape her in her work. She adds: "I am slowly learning that loving people is a key." I love that Margaret says she is "slowly learning": both good words. That's the way it normally is in a teacher/student, mentor/apprentice relationship, which is what discipleship is at its heart.

"I use my abilities to develop affordable housing with supports because I believe Jesus' call to love my neighbors as myself." —Graham, affordable housing developer

Graham is figuring out what it means to obey Jesus' command to love your neighbor as yourself in one very specific area of Hamilton life. Obedience is one of the keys to discipleship: there it is in practice.

A lot of what people said relates to Jesus' emphasis on the worth and dignity of every individual, which in turn derives from the Old Testament conviction that every human being is created in the image of God. So here's Kevin:

"The key effect [of my discipleship] on my work is the knowledge that all human beings are made in the image and likeness of God." —Kevin, accountant

Did you know that was important for accountants? Well, if the accountant happens to be a disciple of Jesus, yes, it is. And really, for anyone in any job at all.

2. THEY SEE THEIR WORK AS CONTRIBUTING TO THE BUILDING OF GOD'S KINGDOM

The good news Jesus brought was that the kingdom of God was breaking into the world through him. So, not surprisingly, a number of disciples talked about what God's kingdom might look like. Here's Graham again:

"I see my work as helping demonstrate to our world that the kingdom of God is real and now available to live into. If Jesus' crucifixion and resurrection broke the powers' hold on the world, and if I believe that, what I'm doing needs to inspire others to see it too."—Graham, affordable housing developer

"My goal is to seek justice and beauty through my work as an architect. I believe that good design affects us as people. I hope that the spaces I help create speak to people's souls, much like nature can do, to point towards God's hand in my work."—Emma, architect

"I think that being a follower of Jesus helps me to want to work with people—relationships and social justice and working in small steps to make our world better and fairer."—Sarah, civil servant

3. THEY TRY TO USE THEIR GOD-GIVEN GIFTS AND PASSIONS IN THEIR WORK

I noticed too that people refer to their gifts and their passions. God has gifted each of us in different ways to work with him for his kingdom in the world. It's not really surprising when you think about it: God created the world, God created work, God created us. So of course these things fit together!

"I sought after work in which my God-given interests met a hunger in the world. I knew working with women and children would be part of it."—Jenna, midwife

"Eventually recognizing my own God-given skills and abilities is what led me to become a psychotherapist."—Steve, counselor

"I have always felt a passion to advocate for people and help people to navigate complicated situations. Given that I work with people who are in a state of crisis, I think I am able to show the gospel of Christ by being compassionate, acting with integrity and fairness and without judgment."—Cathy A., insurance adjuster

4. THEY USE LOTS OF DIFFERENT WORDS TO DESCRIBE WHAT THEY DO, BUT THEY ALL COME DOWN TO LOVE

"The challenges that have been placed in my life as a wife and mother have enabled me to use my skills to bring hope, justice, comfort, and compassion to families challenged by severe mental health concerns." Cathy B., community development worker

"I have been given an opportunity to convey Christ and his mission here on earth not only through *what* I teach (i.e., the content), but also through *how* I teach (e.g., with compassion, concern for the whole person, spiritual discernment, etc.)."—Rosalee, educator

"I deal directly with clients who are often in crisis due to being injured or having lost their jobs. I spend a lot of time listening, problem solving, and encouraging clients. I try to help a client make the best of a difficult situation. I try to be patient, understanding and supportive and at the same time honest about the challenges our clients will have to face."—Mary, litigation law clerk

5. GOD'S LOVE AND CREATIVITY COME THROUGH THEM: THEY ARE JUST PASSING IT ON

Some remind us that this is not just our effort. The work of God's kingdom is, in the first place, God's work, and we can only take part in it when we have experienced something of God's work in our own lives. Otherwise it just wears us out. Here's Cathy B., a community development worker:

"The ways in which I have experienced God's love have led me to want to share God's love and bring hope to others."

God's love for Cathy comes first: then Cathy can pass it on to others. In quite a different kind of work, Brent shows us the same thing:

"I'm drawn to the creativity of our creator, the dizzying complexity and amazing abilities of his creations . . . I just try to make sure that my faith and abilities as a reflection of the creator shine through."—Brent, creative writer

The creativity of the Creator inspires Brent; in his work, he tries to be a reflection of the Creator. I actually think every kind of work is a unique opportunity to show the world what God is like, to be a reflection of God's character. Isn't there something Jesus-like in the work of a garbage collector, or a server at a table in a restaurant, or an actuary?

Here's an interesting question. Do these people consider what they are doing a vocation, a calling? Some people weren't sure.

6. THEIR WORK IS A VOCATION, A CALLING, FROM GOD

Lots of people do see their work as a calling and vocation:

"Of course!! I'm definitely not in it for the money, or because it is easy. It is all about calling."—Emma, architect

"It is definitely a vocation."—Sarah, civil servant

"I do feel called into the work. The job of protecting the transition from expectation to birth as safe and sacred is my passion."—Jenna, midwife

"I felt that I was called to be a teacher, therefore the job was a vocation for me, which I loved."—Adrienne, retired teacher

"For me, my vocation is less about what my 'paid' work is and more about who God has called me to be in the world."—Bethany, professor of community worker outreach and development

"Teaching music was a vocation for me. I followed different paths but focused on this area in my late 30s."—Susan, retired music teacher

"I think I have to consider it a vocation. Quite simply, I have arrived here, and can do this job, only through God's help."—Sharon, drama professor

"I have always understood my job to be the way that I reflect Jesus in the world. I have always felt that it is a vocation and that means it does more than pay the bills—it is a form of worship because it celebrates Jesus in this big part of how I spend my time every day. It is a calling because I sometimes have to prioritize it over other things."—Beth, education consultant

So discipleship in everyday life is not just for religious professionals like me. God has given each of us gifts and passions to serve him in the work of the kingdom. And whatever our job, God can work in us and through us to represent him and the ways of the kingdom in the world.

Let's stop thinking of jobs in a hierarchy, with "spiritual" in the top half and "secular" in the bottom half. Let's get rid of the list altogether. Instead, let's think of it like this: Jesus proclaims the kingdom, calls people to the community of disciples we call the church, and then sends those disciples out to work with him in building the kingdom according to our different gifts.

Have you ever wondered why Redeemer University, up the road from here, is so-called? You may think, "Well, it's just one of the many titles we give Jesus—Savior, Lord, Teacher, Judge, and Redeemer." But no, it's more than that. It's precisely because of what we've been talking about this morning: Redeemer is so called because Jesus Christ is Lord of all of life, not just the religious bits, and he wants to redeem not just human beings, but everything he has created.

That is God's purpose for our world—to redeem and renew all things—and it's the work that disciples are being apprenticed in. There is no higher privilege for a human being than this—to work with the Redeemer of the world as his apprentices. And to hope, at the end of the day, for his words, "Well done, good and faithful servant."

D

Sermons for Special Occasions

WEDDINGS AND FUNERALS ARE almost a weekly duty for ministers of local congregations. For those of us who are occasional preachers, such things happen, well, occasionally. And those occasions are almost always connected with people we know, which puts a certain extra pressure on the preparation—in a good way. So this section includes a wedding and two funerals of people close to me.

The other occasions that follow are also to do with special gatherings, most of them conferences. When I was Director of the Institute of Evangelism, such opportunities came along from time to time. There is also a talk I gave at a camp reunion, as well as the sermon from a rather intimidating service in the college chapel at which I was asked to preach.

16

A Homily for the Wedding of Anna and Benjamin

John 2:1–12

PREACHING AT A WEDDING *is always a treat, but it is a special honor to be asked to preach at the wedding of one's child. I really only have one wedding sermon, but (to be honest) I do feel it's a good one, so I didn't think my daughter suffered from the fact that this had been practiced a few times before her wedding in the summer of 2003. (When my son got married, of course, then I really did have to think of a new one.)*

Scholars are quick to point out that this story is not really about a wedding, but a sign (John's word) of what Jesus does to all of life. In the context of John's Gospel, I think that's quite correct. But then, "all of life" may mean more than weddings but it certainly includes weddings.

Jesus went to a lot of parties, but there is only one story of him going to a wedding reception—and that was nearly a disaster. His mother, Mary, was probably the first to be invited. She seems to have had some responsibility at the reception, so perhaps she was a friend of the family. I wonder if perhaps Jesus and his friends were only invited at the last minute—"Oh sure, if Jesus is in the area, it'd be great to have him"—and that's what caused the problem. We don't know.

At first, everything went well. They were a delightful couple. The service went smoothly, people laughed and cried at the right moments, the food at the reception was perfectly catered. And then, just as they were getting around to the toasts, it happened. "Waiter, would you take the wine round again and then we'll get going on the speeches."

The caterers scurried to open new bottles, but there were none. Not one. They began to panic.

"Have you looked everywhere?"

"You placed the order."

"You've been giving them too much."

"Well, we didn't expect those thirteen extras at the end table, did we? And you know what those fishermen are like: they drink like fish."

"What on earth are we going to do?"

Mary noticed what was happening, and went to Jesus. "Jesus, they've run out of wine."

His answer is strange. It almost sounds callous: "Mother, is that my problem or yours?"

It's as though Jesus is reminding her that these days he has a new set of priorities.

Mary takes the hint. She goes back to the servants: "Listen, if Jesus tells you to do something, even if it seems (she hesitates) weird, just do it. OK?"

"Er, yes, ma'am."

And almost immediately, Jesus calls the servants over. "See those six water-pots by the door? I want you to fill them with water, straight away."

They look at each other sideways, remember what Mary just said, shrug their shoulders, and do it. It's better than doing nothing.

Now these are not regular water pitchers as we know them. These are huge jars that stand three feet from the floor and hold nearly a hundred liters of water each.

Finally they're done.

"OK, sir, it's done."

"Great," says Jesus. Then, with a mischievous twinkle in his eye: "What I want you to do next is this: take a couple of pitchers, fill them from those pots, and take them straight up to the head table." He sees the look on their faces, and chuckles. "And don't worry. It'll be OK. Go on. They're waiting. Trust me!"

And to our surprise, they do it, with fear and trembling, I suspect. Drinking toasts with water was about as popular then as it would be now.

"About time too," says the emcee. "What on earth have you been up to out there—growing the grapes? Anyway, let's just taste this new stuff before you serve everybody. Hmmm. Not bad. In fact, that's pretty good. In fact, fill my glass this time. Yesss. Hey, bridegroom, Benjamin, what are you up to? That first lot of wine was fine. You really didn't need to spend more money on this second batch. This is wonderful stuff. I do believe you've kept the best wine till now. OK, everybody, raise your glasses and let's drink a toast."

As people clink their glasses, the servants stop holding their breath. Mary smiles at Jesus with gratitude, and with something else too. Who is this man who was once her little boy?

The disciples nudge each other: "See what he did? That's amazing! What do you reckon he's going to do next—turn the potato salad into caviar?"

And Jesus winks at the servants. "Well done, you guys."

What's going on here? I notice four things about that wedding, and I want to suggest four things we might pray for this one:

1. JESUS IS SAYING HE'S IN FAVOR OF MARRIAGE

As the old Anglican Prayer Book of 400 years ago said, "This holy estate [of matrimony] Christ adorned and beautified with his presence and first miracle." Marriage has a pretty significant place in God's world. Good marriages make God's world a better place—richer, more joyful, more hospitable, more stable—for all of us. What's more, when people love each other in marriage, we get a glimpse of how God loves us and how we are invited to love God back. I have no hesitation in saying that Jesus is delighted at what is going on here today.

Our prayer for you, Benjamin and Anna, is that you will know the presence of Jesus in your life together every day, and that you will know his pleasure in you and your relationship every day.

2. THEIR WINE RAN OUT

Well, you know what? The wine always runs out in the end. Human resources by themselves are just like that: things do run out, they dry up, they die. Only Jesus can make everything new. Why? Because he is the Creator—and that's what creators do! Without Jesus, we can only do so much. But with Jesus, our lives are infinitely renewable.

People who've been married twenty, thirty, forty years will tell you there are times when the wine runs out, times when you think, "Who on earth is this stranger across the breakfast table? How come I married the most irritating person on the planet?" The thing seems dead. But then, at least sometimes, they find the strength to keep going, and the love returns.

And whether they know it or not, that new life is because of the boundless vitality of Jesus, who can't be stopped—even by death.

Our prayer for you, Anna and Benjamin, is that Jesus will supernaturally renew the resources you need to make your marriage work: love in the form of gentleness and humor, love in the form of forgiveness and patience, love in the form of humility and creativity, day by day, year by year, decade by decade.

3. JESUS' INTENTION IS TO BRING JOY INTO THE WORLD AND INTO OUR LIVES

John's biography of Jesus, from which this story comes, says a lot about the fact that religion kills, with its endless rules and regulations, but that Jesus brings life. That's why, in this biography in particular, Jesus is against religion, and in the end of course he's killed by religious people, because they're scared of what he's saying.

John's biography is also full of symbolism and metaphor. So he wants us to notice what's going on here. For John, these are not just water jars! After all, they were there for a religious ritual of purification. By using them to make wine, Jesus in effect thumbs his nose at the ritual, and says, "Come on, folks, celebrating a wedding with good wine is more fun than washing your hands, isn't it?" And he makes—you worked it out, right?—six lots of 100 liters: 600 liters of outstandingly good wine. Do you think it's possible he's trying to make a point? To be my follower, says Jesus, doesn't mean being a religious weirdo: it's like accepting an invitation to God's party, the best party of all time.

Our prayer for you, Benjamin and Anna, is that you would remain serious followers of Jesus all of your lives, and that, even in the hard times, that commitment would bring you life and joy.

4. BUT PERHAPS THE MOST SIGNIFICANT LINE IN THIS STORY IS MARY'S FIVE SIMPLE WORDS: "DO WHATEVER HE TELLS YOU"

When you think about it, if she hadn't said that, and if the servants hadn't done it, none of the rest would have happened. They wouldn't have filled the water jars; they certainly wouldn't have risked making fools of themselves by offering the emcee water for the toasts. (Try it some time.) But they decided to do whatever Jesus told them. And their obedience somehow created the space in which Jesus could work his miracle.

If we want our water turned to wine, we need to do whatever Jesus tells us. When your marriage is flat as water because you've had a fight, or because you're bored, or because you're not communicating well (and all of those things will happen), obeying Jesus is the key to turning that water into wine once again. Psychiatrist Scott Peck says, "couples sooner or later always fall out of love, and it is at [that] moment . . . that the opportunity for genuine love begins."[1] And that real kind of loving is something Jesus specializes in, so when he asks us to do what he says, his intention is that his disciples will become better lovers.

Our prayer for you, Anna and Benjamin, is that you will do whatever Jesus tells you, even if it's hard, or sounds stupid, or makes you look foolish.

To some, of course, getting married itself is a foolish thing to do these days. But to us who are your guests today, friends and family, your marriage, Benjamin and Anna, is already like wine that gladdens our hearts. May it continue to gladden the hearts of all who come into contact with you.

---

1. Peck, *Road Less Traveled*, 118.

17

My Mother's Funeral

WE ALWAYS KNOW—IN THEORY, at least—that our parents will die. And my mother had been in slow decline in her eighties for some years. As a result, I became aware that I was half-consciously preparing to speak at her funeral for a long time before it actually happened, in October 2003.

Part of the challenge was not knowing the audience (the first thing I always want to know about a sermon—even before I know the text). But I could guess at some things. Some present would be her contemporaries, a diminishing number, who had been going to church with her for years. I wanted to encourage them. Others were family or other friends with no church connection whatsoever. How to say something which would honor her, and at the same time not be so "religious" as to turn off the nonchurch folk—that was the challenge. For them, my hope was to sow a seed in their minds, a fresh way of thinking about faith that might in time bear fruit. This sermon is what I came up with. I like to think she would be pleased.

As some of you know, I am a layperson teaching in an Anglican theological college in Toronto—which I guess makes me what you could call a lay theologian. And I come by this honestly, because Mum was also a lay theologian. This may sound strange, but theology is not done by old men thinking deep thoughts about God in book-lined studies. Basically, every Christian is a theologian, in the sense that you think about God and the things you hear from the Bible in relation to the things that happen in your life and the things you read in the newspaper. And the conclusions you come to about God and about life are actually theology, just as surely as those deep thoughts of the old guy in the university are theology. Sometimes moreso.

So Mum was a theologian, though she'd be surprised to hear me say so. Let me tell you three theological reflections I heard from her over the years which have stuck with me and which seem particularly relevant today.

Number one. I remember, when I was very small, I'd gone to bed before my father came home from a meeting, and for some reason I got worried about the fact that Dad hadn't come home when he said he would, so I went down to tell Mum I was scared. I don't remember much of what she said, but I do remember her saying, "John, we just have to trust God." And I would say that attitude towards life, of saying, "I will trust God whatever happens," stayed with her over the years.

Of course, for all of us who try to be Christians, there are things which shake our faith, and times when we say to God, I will never be able to trust you again. (In our family life, there was a day when Dad did not come home from a meeting, but Mum continued to trust God anyway.) But for myself, I have tried to keep that attitude of trusting God whatever happens, finding that life makes more sense that way.

For instance, if God has set the world up as a gymnasium where we can be trained to be spiritually strong, then we shouldn't expect it to be easy or fair, and difficulties should not surprise us. So I find I can shout at God, and be angry with God, and complain at the mess he lets the world get into, but at the end of the day, I still trust a loving God who gives me hope when there is no other reason for hope. Thanks, Mum.

Number two. Perhaps I was twelve or thirteen, but I have a vague memory that a number of families around us who had always gone to church stopped going, within quite a short period of time. But Mum, of course, kept going, and so we did too. And she said to me, "I feel that going to church is part of our witness." And she was right.

I teach courses about evangelism—which doesn't mean how to be a TV evangelist, you may be glad to know, but how to help churches become warm, welcoming places where people can comfortably explore their spirituality, ask their questions, and grow into faith. But if that's evangelism, evangelism needs witness to make it credible: and by witness I mean the day in, day out, quiet, consistent living out of the Christian faith—going to church, certainly, but also going the second mile for someone, forgiving someone who is frankly unforgiveable, giving time to someone others have no time for. That's witness. Someone has said a witness is a signpost: not especially valuable in itself, but invaluable because it points you in the direction of somewhere you want to go. And Mum was a witness to her Christian faith. Thanks, Mum.

Number three. I suppose I must have been preparing for confirmation (that ritual by which young people publicly declare their intention never to go to church again), and I was talking to her about what we were discussing. We were talking about that phrase in the creed, "I believe in the resurrection of the body," and she said, "I think it would be better to say, the resurrection of a body." What she meant was that life in the next world is not in the body we have now (anyone over forty will be glad to know that) but in a new body. Theologians (the professional and the lay kind) say the prototype for this is the body of Jesus after the resurrection: the disciples knew it was him, he could talk with them, he could have a meal with them, they could give him a hug—and yet he was different. It often took them a little time to realize it really was him, and he could appear and disappear at will, for example. So Jesus had a body at that point, but not exactly the body he had before.

So I think Mum was right. I don't think we'll advertise it too widely, because people have died to defend little words like "the" and "a" in documents like the creed. But I am encouraged to know that Mum's body in the next life will not be the worn-out body that finally stopped working on Tuesday morning, but one that in some mysterious way will express the person she really was—really is—so that when we see her, we will say, "Betty, you're looking so much more yourself than when we saw you last." I'm looking forward to that. Thanks, Mum.

18

The Funeral of My Canadian Mother

Romans 8:18–39

WE ALL HAVE OUR heroes, and Joyce was one of mine. She was not much taller than five feet, and came from Holland to Canada after the Second World War. There, as a single mother, she raised six children, five boys (one with severe mental disabilities) and one girl. Most of the boys were over six feet tall, and three became Presbyterian ministers.

When she was seventy years old, I was in need of a secretary, and one of her sons suggested she might like the job. She was wonderful, and served not only as secretary but as mother-figure to the IVCF staff in the area—not least to me. Once during that time, my biological mother visited from Wales, and they spent a day together. I never did enquire what they talked about, but they said they had a good time.

Joyce died in the summer of 2015, having not quite reached a hundred. The service took place at St. Paul's Presbyterian Church in Ottawa, Ontario, Joyce's home church for many years, and I was honored to be the preacher.

May my words glorify God and honor the memory of our mother, grandmother, great-grandmother, and friend, Joyce.

The Bible is no stranger to death and grief and sadness and loss—the things that are pressing on us today. They are dark threads that run through the whole Bible from almost the first chapter to almost the final chapter. But the Bible is equally insistent that death and grief and sadness and loss do not have the last word in our world. There is a power at work in our world that is greater than any of those things—the unstoppable love of God through Jesus Christ which is able to make everything new, and which will win in the end.

One of the places that triumph of God's love is clearest in the Bible is in Paul's letter to the Romans from which we've heard readings today because it was one of Joyce's favorite parts of the Bible. Some of us remember her ninetieth birthday party here in this church. When it was time for her to make a speech, she got out her Bible, opened it to the book of Romans, and said (and I won't try to imitate her accent), "Some people think Romans is difficult to understand. I think it's perfectly straightforward." And she proceeded to read and then expound chapter 5 to her birthday guests. Which is one reason I'm not going to presume to talk about that chapter today.

Instead, I want to think about chapter 8, and I'm going to start right in the middle, where Paul shares his God-given vision for the future of our world. I don't know what picture comes to your mind when you think about the future of the world. Paul uses an image I can guarantee doesn't come spontaneously to anyone's mind. Picking up on something Jesus said, he says it's as if our world is pregnant, and that the hard times the world is going through are actually the groans of a world in labor. (Eugene Peterson translates it, "The difficult times of pain throughout the world are simply birth pangs" [Rom 8:22 MSG].)

But if that's so, we want to know, what is it the world is going to give birth to, according to Paul? Simply this: a new world where sin and death, suffering and evil—those things that weigh on us, to one extent or another, every day, not just on days like today—are all done away with.

Now, you may roll your eyes at that and say, "Come on, this is just wishful thinking, it's pie in the sky when you die, just the sort of thing you expect to hear at a funeral. Don't expect us to believe it." Well, Paul is aware of that question, it's just that he's not dealing with it in this part of Romans. In the places where he does discuss it, his argument is that this vision is rooted in solid historical fact, specifically the reality of Jesus, his death, and resurrection. If you want to know the rational basis for this vision, that's where to look and do your research.

But, perhaps surprisingly, the birth of this new world is in one way dependent on us. Paul says God is waiting for us to be ready before bringing the rest of this new world into being. In fact, he uses another image—he says the created world is standing on tiptoe, anxiously trying to get a glimpse of how we're doing. (Of course, quite how you could be in labor and standing on tiptoe at the same time is not clear, but Paul does sometimes mix his metaphors.)

Why is the world looking to us? Maybe it's because we are further away from God than the natural world, so we have some catching up to do. Or maybe it's because God trusted us to be stewards of the world, and we have messed that up pretty badly, and creation is waiting to see if we can get our act together, for us to become the Christlike servant leaders God always intended us to be.

Either way, how are we getting ready for this new world? One way is in verse 28: "in all things God works for the good of those who love him." Here's that verse again, in Peterson's words: "Every detail of our lives, of love for God, is worked into something good." Not that God is playing favorites: "Hah, you love me, so I'll be nice to you." No, it's just that, if you are trying to love God, you'll be open to God doing things in your life. And, frankly, if you don't want God to mess around in your life, it's not wise to get too close to him.

The thought that a loving God can turn all things to good is amazing, isn't it? All things? Apparently so. Even the death of someone we love very much, and the feelings of grief and sadness and loss that follow? Absolutely. That's how those things don't have the last word.

Certainly those things can push people further away from God, but what God is able to do (if we are open) is to use those things to strengthen our spiritual muscles and reinforce our commitment to God's work in the world—in other words, God will use those negative things for our good. The saying, "What doesn't kill you makes you stronger" is not in the Bible—though some think it comes from Hezekiah 3:16—but in the hands of God the personal trainer that's how it can be.

So just what is it that God is training us for? It's in the next verse (29): "to shape the lives of those who love (God) along the same lines as the life of his son (Jesus)." To put it another way, God's intention for us is not that we should be religious and weird (though there are certainly some Christians who might make you wonder). No, God's intention is simply this: to make us fully human, as Jesus was fully human—fully alive, fully reflecting the beauty of God in the world. As one theologian many centuries ago put it: the glory of God is a human being fully alive!

So, here's how Paul summarizes his argument this far (30): "After God made that decision of what his children should be like (like Jesus), he followed it up by calling people by name. After he called them by name, he set them on a solid basis with himself. And then, after getting them established, he stayed with them to the end, gloriously completing what he had begun."

Would it be pushing it too far to apply these words to Joyce—or indeed to any of us who are seeking to follow Jesus? It would sound like this: "After God made that decision of what Joyce should be like, he followed it up by calling her by name. After he called Joyce by name, he set her on a solid basis with himself.

And then, after getting her established, he stayed with Joyce to the end, gloriously completing what he had done." I think that works, don't you?

The chapter then ends with seven rhetorical questions, seven glorious and victorious trumpet blasts:

1. What shall we say in response to these things?
2. If God is for us, who can be against us?
3. He who did not spare his own Son, how will he not also, along with him, graciously give us all things?
4. Who will bring any charge against those whom God has chosen?
5. Who then is the one who condemns? No one.
6. Who shall separate us from the love of Christ?
7. Shall trouble or hardship or persecution or famine or nakedness or danger or sword? (All of them things that threaten death!) And the answer is a resounding No!

Paul says in effect: Look, if this is the plan that almighty God is carrying out, to abolish death and sadness and loss, this plan to create a new world, and to begin with the renewal of human beings, nothing can stand in its way, what on earth are you worried about?

The Message says, "Nothing fazes us because Jesus loves us" (Rom 8:37) The older versions say, "In all these things—however difficult, however sad—we are more than conquerors (a difficult Greek word to translate, because Paul made up a new word—super-conquerors!)—not because we are such wonderful people but—through him who loved us." In fact, it shouldn't surprise us that three times in these last five verses Paul mentions love: the love of Christ (35), him who loved us (37), and the love of God in Christ (39).

Do you detect a theme here? Of course: it's the love of God channeled to us through Christ that anchors this picture of God's new world in reality. Nothing else could possibly be big enough or strong enough to bear the weight of such a vision.

It has been said that the most important question we can ever ask is: What is God like? And the Bible's answer is that God the Creator is always at work to put right all that we have put wrong in the world; that this God came to the world uniquely in Jesus Christ to begin the decisive phase of his restoration project; and that men and women are invited to be part of this new thing God is doing, and to find meaning and life and joy in doing so.

This is the God of Jesus and his apostles, the God of Paul, the God of Christians down the centuries, and the God of Joyce. And we are invited to make this God our God too.

19

The Day the Archbishop Came to Chapel

John 17:1–11

ROWAN WILLIAMS BECAME ARCHBISHOP of Canterbury in 2002. That was a period when Anglican churches throughout the world—the Anglican Communion—were struggling with questions of human sexuality. The majority of North America Anglicans advocated changes to doctrine, liturgy, and attitude, while the growing church of the Global South held strongly to traditional views. The Archbishop of Canterbury is not an Anglican pope, but rather the senior leader of the Communion in a spiritual and pastoral sense, which made Rowan Williams's role uniquely difficult. It was said of a previous incumbent of the office, "he had nailed his colours to the fence"[1]—meaning, it is the job of the Archbishop of Canterbury not to assert his own personal views, but to hold all sides together. To a remarkable extent, Dr Williams succeeded in this impossible task.

During this period, in April 2007, he visited Wycliffe College. One item in the schedule was chapel, and I was invited to preach. There were many topics I would have been happy to preach on (maybe one of those familiar "signature sermons"), but the gospel reading appointed for the day was from John 17, Jesus' high-priestly prayer for unity among Christians. I suppose I could have

---

1. Shortt, *Rowan's Rule*, 6.

dodged the bullet and chosen another text, but I felt that doing so would have been cowardly and probably disobedient. God's strange sense of humor again. Nobody in their right minds wants to preach on Christian unity these days. It's too easy to fall into the traps of platitudes on the one hand and good advice on the other—neither of which we need. But if it shows up in the lectionary, which it did today, what are you supposed to do?

This prayer of Jesus in John 17, of which we heard the first part, actually reminds me of a rock, black and solid, rising out of the middle of a stormy sea. And I say that because of the context in which it is set.

Recall what's happened already in this part of John. It began with the washing of the disciples' feet in chapter 13. What more beautiful moment of unity could there have been? But Peter blows it: "Lord, I don't want you washing my feet. That's not right. Come on!" And the moment's gone.

Then there's the Passover meal, a time for the family to come together and to celebrate their unity and their diversity. But this time it's Judas who destroys the moment: he gets up, leaves the table, and goes out into the night. And what unity there was is spoiled.

Then there is that long section of teaching, from the end of chapter 13 to the end of chapter 16. I imagine them all listening intently, trying to take it all in, sitting on the edge of their—well, I guess not, but you know what I mean—and John, madly scribbling, trying to get it all down because otherwise people will think he made it up. And this time it's Philip: "Jesus, this is all very well, but why don't you just show us the father: that's all we need really."

And Jesus sighs: "Philip, you just don't get it, do you?"

At the end of chapter 16, finally things seem to be coming together. The disciples say, in effect, "Thank you, Jesus, we finally get it. You've dropped all that difficult parable stuff we never did understand. We believe!" You can almost feel the euphoria in the room: finally, they are united.

But this time it's Jesus who pricks the unity bubble. "Folks, don't get too excited: before long, you're going to abandon me and scatter."

And they're all deflated.

The prayer in chapter 17 comes after all that. And the irony is that the theme of unity is absolutely central. In fact, it becomes louder and more insistent as the chapter goes on. He prays for his followers to be united as the Father and the Son are united. (No pressure, eh?) This kind of unity would fulfill God's image in us, it would be God's glory in human beings fully alive, it would be for all the world to see and be in awe of and be drawn to. It's an amazing picture—but of course it is only a picture.

Because then chapter 18 returns us to what we like to call the real world. They go to the garden: Judas comes with the soldiers, Peter lops off

Malchus's ear, and they take Jesus to Caiaphas. The disciples scatter as Jesus said they would. Then, to make things worse, Peter betrays Jesus.

In chapters 13 to 16, at least there were glimpses of unity: now there is nothing. In fact, the only people who are really united are the enemies of Jesus, who demonstrate in an extraordinary way how a community can be united in diversity. Too bad they do it for the wrong reasons.

You see why I think of this prayer as a rock, rising dark and lonely above the storms and chaos of the chapters round about it.

I begin to think this prayer is only going to be answered eschatologically. That's not to let us off the hook. We still have to work at unity. But it's also to say that it shouldn't surprise us when Christians are not united, and we should be grateful for any glimpses we can catch in the here-and-now.

For twentysomething years, my wife and I worked at a summer camp. And, although (as some here know to their cost) I'm not a morning person, my favorite time of the day used to be early morning, especially towards the end of the summer, when the sun was not quite up yet, and there was a mist on the lake and nobody else was around except a family of loons. Perhaps you know places like that.

Now if the fog lasted all day (as it did occasionally), we'd get very tired of it. But usually we could put up with it because we knew that, in half an hour, when we got that first blessed cup of coffee, the sun would be up, and the fog would have burned off.

In our world and in our church (as in these chapters), there's a lot of fog around—the fog of foolishness and unfaithfulness and failure. We are all traitors to Jesus, one way or another.

But there are also glimpses through the fog of great beauty—moments when we see disciples of Jesus united, in worship or in mission or in study, across ethnic lines or denominational lines or linguistic lines (you've seen it and so have I)—and, even more amazing, sometimes we even get to be the catalyst in helping such things come about, and we say, "Yes, that's it. That's how it was meant to be. That's what he was praying for. See—it can happen."

But then before long the fog rolls in again, the glimpse seems like a mirage, and we begin to doubt whether the sun will ever rise. But I take heart from the fact that Jesus prayed this, and prayed it repeatedly, and intensely, and at this crucial moment in his life (when he could have been praying for a thousand other things).

It tells me this: the fog is not the final reality: the beauty of the unity of the people of God will win in the end. And of that the guarantee is the word and the prayer of Jesus Christ himself. Thanks be to God.

20

An Evangelist among the Scientists

Your Jesus is Too Small (Colossians 1:15–20)

I AM NOT A scientist, and haven't studied science since high school. So I was rather surprised, though honored, to be asked to preach at the Sunday service during the annual conference of Christians in science. This brought together two academic groups, the American Scientific Affiliation and the Canadian Scientific and Christian Affiliation. The conference took place at McMaster University, not far from where I live, in July 2014. As I thought about a suitable text, I was helped by recalling that the historic motto of McMaster is "In Christ all things hold together," though it is not referred to very much these days. Then I thought, Well, "all things" obviously includes the sciences. Since the title of the conference was From Cosmos to Psyche: All Things Hold Together in Christ, I am guessing the organizers thought the same. This is the result.

The sermon was later published in the journal of the ASA, Perspectives on Science and Christian Faith—I think I can say with confidence the first and last time I will have an article in a scientific journal.

Some sixty years ago, J. B. Phillips, the Bible translator, wrote a book called, *Your God is Too Small*. It was about our tendency to shrink God to manageable proportions, but I think Paul might say not only that our God is too small but our Jesus is too small. Paul is writing Colossians to Christians who think they need to supplement their worship of Jesus with other things—with religion and ritual and philosophy—a kind of "Jesus-plus" spirituality.

And Paul says "No, no, if you think that, you haven't really understood Jesus yet." So he's trying to set the record straight, and the heart of his argument is here in Colossians 1. And part of that argument is the theme of your conference, which is also the historic motto of McMaster University: "In Christ all things hold together."

It's an amazing vision, isn't it? Paul somehow sees that the carpenter of Nazareth is also the one who made absolutely everything and who holds absolutely everything together. It is this Jesus who gives coherence and meaning to everything that exists. This Jesus holds together the atoms in our bodies, keeps the laws of physics constant, and keeps the distant stars in their courses. When we do our work, it is this Jesus who keeps our brain functioning, this Jesus whose world we are exploring, this Jesus whose truths we are discovering. It is even this Jesus who enables our brains to doubt whether he exists.

It would be interesting to know whether John and Paul ever had a conversation and, if they did, to know what they said to each other. They would have had a lot to talk about, not least because both have a huge understanding of who Jesus is. I imagine Paul saying, "I like to think of him as holding all things together."

John says, "I've been thinking about that too. In fact, I'm thinking of writing a biography of Jesus, and I think I might call him the Logos. I'm sure you know the idea—it crops up in so many religions and philosophies these days—that there's a rational principle behind the universe. And of course you and I know the name of that rational principle."

And Paul says, "Shoot, I wish I'd thought of that."

But if we put these two things together—the Jesus whom Paul says holds all things together, and the Jesus John calls the Logos, the creative mind of God become flesh—then every discipline that ends in -ology is a whimsical reminder of the centrality, the bigness, of Jesus Christ. He is the logos in cosm-ology, ge-ology, bi-ology, entom-ology, biotechn-ology, climat-ology, zo-ology, kinesi-ology, even paleoanthrop-ology (a new one to me, though represented at this conference). And because Jesus is at the heart of all our work, whatever our discipline (whether or not it ends in -ology!), that gives us hope and purpose and meaning that (frankly) is very difficult to find anywhere else.

This is why "All things together—all things cohering—in Christ" makes such a great motto for a university. It says that, whatever our discipline, whether humanities or social sciences or sciences, we are all engaged in the same project, and there is an overarching coherence to all we do. All of us are seeking to think God's thoughts after him, in all their diversity and beauty and complexity. Whatever our discipline, we know that "all truth is God's truth"—because Jesus Christ is holding the universe together. Hence, of course, the word "university." Without that, we are just a polyversity or a multiversity. No wonder it's hard replacing Christian mottos with secular ones for universities these days. How do you express the rationale of the institution in a single phrase when there is no unifying principle, no sense that all knowledge is part of some greater whole? A motto like "Try harder" really doesn't cut it.

But Paul didn't write Colossians to justify the use of the word "university." He has bigger fish to fry. So in verse 18, as N. T. Wright points out, Paul moves from talking about creation to talking about new creation.[1] We can't stop at saying that Christ created all things and that Christ holds all things together. There's more.

In the verses which follow, Paul talks about Christ's incarnation ("in him all the fullness of God was pleased to dwell" [19]), about his atoning death ("making peace by the blood of his cross" [20]), and his resurrection ("the firstborn from the dead" [18]). And what is the purpose of those things? It is "so that he might come to have first place in everything" (18).

But, we might wonder, if Christ created all things and Christ upholds all things, surely he has first place in everything already? But of course Paul is thinking of sin, and the fact that this is a fallen world, where we do not see Christ supreme much of the time. And the purpose of his incarnation and death and resurrection is precisely so that supremacy which is rightfully his might be restored. Or, to put it Paul's way, "through him God was pleased to reconcile to himself all things, whether on earth or in heaven" (20). Ultimately, God is about the renewal of the cosmos—not content with forgiving our sins, cleaning up our lives, and renewing us by his Spirit. God is concerned to redeem, restore, and renew all things (the word "all" is used eight times in just six verses)—our relationships, neighborhoods, cities, cultures, work, and all the ways the natural world has been hurt by the evil of human beings. It's as though the redeeming work of God through Jesus is a series of ripples spreading out and out from the cross until they embrace the whole of creation.

I love the way Eugene Peterson translates this part:

> He was supreme in the beginning, and, leading the resurrection parade, he is supreme in the end. From beginning to end he's there, towering far above everything, everyone. So spacious is he, so roomy, that everything of God finds its proper place in

---

1. Wright, *Epistles of Paul*, 73.

him without crowding. Not only that, but all the broken pieces of the universe—people and things, animals and atoms—get properly fixed and fit together in vibrant harmonies, all because of his death, his blood that poured down from the cross (18b–20 MSG).

But there's a word just before this that jars me, and maybe you too: it's the word "church": "He is the head of the body, the church" (18a). Maybe it jars because these days it has such negative connotations in our world. But of course, when Paul says "church," he doesn't have in mind what we often associate with church; he means something which fits perfectly into this vision of Christ. What then does he mean?

One of the most helpful ways of thinking about church comes from New Testament scholar N. T. Wright. He's suggested the Bible is like a five-act play—although (as Richard Middleton and Brian Walsh have pointed out) it works better if we think of it as a six-act play.

- Act 1 is the story of creation: God creates a beautiful and fruitful world, and entrusts it to our care.
- Act 2 is the story of what has gone wrong in our world: we decide that we know how to run it better than the Creator.
- Act 3 is the story of the Old Testament: that God, in love, begins over, starting with Abraham and Sarah and the promise that, through their descendants, blessing will be restored to the whole world. Everywhere sin has done its dirty work, the redeeming work of God is sure to follow.
- And then, in act 4, the Creator writes himself into the script—as if Shakespeare should write himself into the plot of *Hamlet*, so that Hamlet could get to know his Creator. And when the Creator appears on the stage, he shows us what a fully human life is like, he dies for our sins, he rises from death, and he returns to heaven. And we call his name Jesus.
- Finally, act 6 is when the creator rings down the curtain on this drama at the end of time, when God's work of dealing with sin, evil, and brokenness is complete, and the new heaven and the new earth are ushered in.

So what is act 5? This is where we are now, the time between Christ's first coming (in act 4) and his second coming (in act 6), the age of the church. There is no script for act 5: we need to exercise faithful improvization—living as the people of God in contexts the biblical writers never envisioned, and yet being faithful to the spirit and the direction of the story as we have received it.

How does the church fit, right there in the middle of Paul's glorious vision? Because at its heart, church is the community of those called by God to work with him in the redemption of the world. I used to say that the church is a community of Jesus' disciples, which it is, but "disciple" is kind of an old-fashioned, religious word. So for a time I used to say that a disciple was a student, but then realized in our culture "student" means someone (generally young) sitting in a desk taking notes from a lecture, which is hardly what Jesus meant. (You probably know the old definition of a lecture: the means by which the lecturer's notes become the student's notes, without passing through the minds of either.)

I have come to think that, these days, a better word than "disciple" is probably "apprentice." The church is the community of apprentices of Jesus. Like any apprentice, we are learning from the master craftsman how to do the things the master does so well—in the case of Christian apprenticeship, we are learning from Jesus, our Teacher, in whatever field we are called, how to do the work of God to restore, renew, and redeem all things. That's why church—with you and me as part of it—is right there in the middle of Paul's vision. We are part of this amazing work of God.

I don't know who you are, but I do know this: that whatever your role in this world—whether professor, researcher, or student, whether physicist, neurobiologist, or medical ethicist, whether it's in an office, a classroom, or a lab, whether beginning your career or ending your career or somewhere in the middle—if you are a disciple, an apprentice, of Jesus Christ, he will work in you and through you—indeed, he is already working in you and through you—to do this work of redeeming, renewing, and restoring all things.

Friends, this is what we were made for, this is worth getting up in the morning for, this is worth giving our all for. Yes, it is the way of suffering and self-sacrifice, certainly—Jesus never promised it would be easy—but it is also the way of joy. And isn't this the heart of the gospel, that through Jesus Christ, his life, death, and resurrection, God is restoring joy to a fallen world? Joy in us, and joy through us and through the church, to the world?

21

A Camp Reunion

The Leaders in Training from 1986

DURING THE YEARS I worked for IVCF Canada, my summer placement was at Ontario Pioneer Camps. Back in 1928, the founder of IVCF, Howard Guinness, could not imagine a student ministry without a summer camp, where students from the universities could be trained in leadership and evangelism.

Howard Guinness's idea was a good one, but he did not know Deborah and me, and we really were not camp people. (I did finally figure out which end of a canoe was the front, but it took a bit.) So what were we any good for? It took three years of trial and error before we landed in the Leader-in-Training program. But once we found it, or it found us, it was a great match. I don't know if there really is a sign in the Australian Outback which says, "Choose your rut carefully, because you could be in it for a long time." But the LIT program was a great rut for us to be stuck in. We stayed for seventeen summers. Each year, I would report to our support community in Ottawa, and say, "I really think this was the best year yet." And our friends would nod and smile indulgently, because they knew I always said that.

Camp, of course, means reunions. Most happen for a year or two after camp is over. But in 2004, my friend Brendan Caldwell decided to organize a reunion of his leadership cohort, and asked me to speak. I had first met Brendan when he was sixteen and an LIT; I had been his small group leader.

Reunions always make you aware of the passing of time. When we began doing the LIT program in 1981, I was thirty-four, twice the age of the LITs; when I stopped in 1997, after seventeen summers, I was fifty-one, three times the age of the LITs—though that's not why I stopped! To be honest, I wanted to keep doing it till my daughter Anna had been through the program, which was in 1996. After all, not every parent has the opportunity to teach their children for eight sessions without interruption, and then have them write an exam at the end, and I wasn't going to pass up the opportunity. Then in 1996, the camp asked if I would go back one more year so they could make a professional video of Building Blocks—which was difficult to say no to.

You were LITs in 1986. The teenagers who were LITs this year (2004) were not even born until 1988, two years later. When you were LITs, my son Ben was ten and at Junior Camp (as it then was) and my daughter Anna was six (in the Grasshoppers program). They are now twenty-nine and twenty-four respectively, did LIT a very long time ago, and are both married and both working. If that makes you feel old, welcome to the club. It gets worse!

I suppose it was partly an awareness of the passing of time that was behind the survey of former LITs that many of you took part in last year—and this is as good a moment as any to say thank you if you did so. You will be interested to know that I'm still working on the data: I do have a publisher, and hopefully the book will be finished and out in the next year.[1]

I suppose I became curious about what happened to LITs because, over the years, I would often meet former LITs, or get news of others, and I would learn that some were doing well and some were not doing well—and that might mean in terms of faith, or of marriage, or career, or whatever. And I began to think: I gave a big chunk of my life to the people in that program. What happened to them all? Was that a good way to spend my summers? Shouldn't I have been doing a real job? How do I feel about the fact that I invested those prime years of my life into those people? What return have I got for that investment?

It's interesting the language we use, isn't it? Investing my life. If we invest, normally we hope for a return on our investment. If we can think of our lives like money, I guess that's a reasonable image. I invest three or four years in getting an education, and the return I get is a degree and understanding or skills in a particular field. There are times when that is a useful way to think.

The problem with the language of investing is that it's not always appropriate. Suppose parents decide to invest in having two or three children.

---

1. This was published in 2010 as *Growing Up Christian*.

What might they expect as a suitable return? That they support their parents in their old age? That they fulfill all the dreams the parents had but couldn't live out? That they carry on the family traditions—whether that's a tradition of faith, or of business, or of the family name? But what if they do none of the above? I suppose there are parents who think, "It's not fair: all those years I slaved for you, paid for you, invested in you—and this is how you repay me?" Meaning, I suppose, it was a quasi-financial agreement, an unwritten business contract, in the first place.

Of course in the West we tend to say, "I don't care what they do as long as they're happy." (Although I'm not sure why we think happiness is the most important thing. I suspect that quite evil people are happy.) The instinct is a good one, I think, to say, "I didn't do this for a reward." There is a word for doing things for other people that don't get a reward: you know what it is? Love.

I don't often think God speaks to me, at least audibly, and you won't often hear me say, "The Lord said to me . . .," but as I began to think about what had happened with the 1,200 LITs we spent time with, I did feel that God said to me, "But you did love them." And I suppose that is true, that I—and all the other leaders of course—did try to love the LITs in spite of all our mixed motives, and our imperfections, and our self-centeredness. We did try to love.

So I find I am less concerned these days to know if the investment of my life is paying off. I'm not sure that's the most important criterion from God's point of view. What God asks of me is: Did you try to love these people? I'm not responsible for what people do with their lives. All I can do is love them as best I can.

Why is this so important? I suppose I'm coming to the conclusion that love is important because it's at the heart of what life is all about—and for that reason it's what Christian faith is about. That kind of love is important because this is what God is like, this is what Jesus is like, this is how God made human beings to be.

It's not that if you're nice, you go to heaven, and if you're nasty, you don't. (I didn't believe that in 1986, and I don't believe it now!) No, salvation is simply God, out of love (this kind of love), offering us a relationship with him, at no cost (at least, no cost to us).

But that's only the beginning, not the end. I remember one family who had adopted two little girls, who were being quite a handful. One day, while I was staying with them, one of them ran into the house and asked her father, "Daddy, was I adopted or adapted?" And the father replied with a wry smile, "Sweetheart, you were adopted: we're still working on the adapting." Being adopted by God costs us nothing; being adapted by God is a lifelong process.

We often hear that the Christian life is a life of discipleship, of learning from Jesus. But what are we learning? The contents of the Bible? A Christian worldview? Answers to difficult ethical questions? Well, maybe. But at the heart of it, we're learning to love, as God loves. Why? Because this is how God's new world will be at the end of time. And we are acclimatizing ourselves to that world. We're making ourselves strong in the ways of that world, so that on that day we will be in our element—like pollywogs growing lungs so that one day they can survive on land.

Here's how C. S. Lewis puts it in *The Four Loves*. (I know you'd be disappointed if he didn't come in somewhere.)

> Natural loves can hope for eternity only in so far as they have allowed themselves to be taken into the eternity of Charity [God's self-giving kind of love]; have at least allowed the process to begin here on earth, before the night comes when no man can work. And the process will always involve a kind of death. There is no escape. In my love for wife or friend the only eternal element is the transforming presence of Love Himself. By that presence, if at all, the other elements may hope, as our physical bodies hope, to be raised from the dead. For this only is holy in them, this only is the Lord.[2]

I didn't think of it at the time, but actually the heart of the LIT program was learning to love—not that we ever said that, as far as I remember. We talked about a lot of things—how to teach canoeing, and how to take care of kids, and how to lead a Bible study, and how to lead a camp song, and what a worldview is, how to clean toilets without complaining, and—of course—about servant leadership. But although it sounds like a lot of different things, I think they're all basically the same thing: they all relate to learning to love.

So what have you been up to since 1986? Some of you have made your first million—and I'm happy for you. Some of you have got married and had children: that's great. Some of you are involved in professional ministry: and that's a good thing. One of you is my financial adviser, and I'm grateful for that. You probably don't remember a lot of what you learned that summer of 1986, and that's OK. (There's no exam this time.) But there is one lesson from that summer I hope you're continuing to learn: I hope you are continuing to learn from the God who invented love, the Scriptures that tell stories of lovers good and bad, and the Jesus who modeled a life of love, how to be a better lover. And, as I'm learning in my own life, that's the most important thing, it's what life is all about.

---

2. Lewis, *Four Loves*, 125.

22

Having the Last Word

Faith for the Future (Hebrews 11:8–12, 17–19)

ONE OF THE HIGHLIGHTS *of my tenure at the Wycliffe College Institute of Evangelism, for me anyway, was the seven Vital Church Planting conferences I directed at St. Paul's Bloor Street in Toronto. Ideas of contextual church planting were just beginning to filter across the Atlantic from Britain, where the movement was called Fresh Expressions. The conferences were an attempt to transplant that DNA into the Anglican Church of Canada. Many people, including bishops and church leaders from numerous other denominations, came from all over Canada, and the gatherings slowly helped to foster new ways of understanding church and mission in many quarters.*

One regular feature of the conferences was that at the closing Eucharist we would hear from a guest preacher. One year (2010), I missed a crucial planning meeting where the name for that year was discussed. This sermon is the result.

You know what happens if you miss a committee meeting? You end up doing jobs everyone else voted for you to do, and you're not there to defend yourself. Two weeks ago, I was sick and missed a planning meeting, and let's just say I didn't volunteer to preach today.

My first thought was, I'm sure I have a knock-'em-dead sermon I've used before that would fit. (You would never think something like that, I know.) Then, the very next day, in my personal Bible reading, I read a passage that just jumped out at me as the right text for this morning. Even the four points (and yes, I do have points) were right there in my face. The passage is Hebrews 11, and in particular the four times it specifically says "By faith, Abraham . . ." (It won't escape your notice that all my four points begin with the same letter: B.)

Here are the four. After these two days of conference, the texts will hardly need comment . . . though I should warn you I'm going to anyway.

1. BY FAITH, ABRAHAM SET OUT, NOT KNOWING WHERE HE WAS GOING (8)

This is counterintuitive, isn't it? You just don't go out without knowing where you're going. You especially don't sell your house, pack up your belongings, and hit the road without knowing where you are going. But Abraham knew this was what he had to do. Hebrews says it was a matter of obedience—not a virtue highly valued these days. But for Hebrews, Abraham isn't doing something weird: this is a just a normal aspect of the life of faith.

The thing that's odd, even eccentric, is to have a five-year plan that tells us exactly where we're going, how we're going to get there, and how much it will cost, including tax, some of which can be reclaimed. Not that God doesn't sometimes bless five-year plans, but they're not really the norm.

Today, with the church where it is, after all we've heard at this conference, this is us: we are called to go out, in the sense of leaving the familiar, the tried-and-true, not knowing where we're going. All we know, as one speaker said, is that "the status quo is not acceptable." Steve Croft, the first Team Leader of Fresh Expressions UK, wrote a report at the end of his five-year tenure, and called it: "There was No Five-Year Plan." For people of faith, like Abraham, that's normal.

2. BY FAITH, ABRAHAM LIVED AS AN IMMIGRANT IN A LAND HE HAD BEEN PROMISED HE WOULD OWN (9)

Abraham had been promised this land—but he did not count ownership of the land a thing to be grasped. He had it on an open palm. He was a sojourner, a *paroikos*, a temporary resident, content to live in tents and move around, and never assert his ownership. In a funny way, our situation in Canada is the opposite. Abraham anticipated owning land; we look back to, well, not owning the land, though we may once have thought we did—our

First Nations brothers and sisters have reminded us of our hubris in ever thinking such a thing—but at least feeling that we as the church had a right to a central place, a place of influence and status, in Canadian society. We haven't had to live in cultural tents on the margins for a long time: our city-center churches and cathedrals speak to that.

But now, like Abraham, we find ourselves a minority on the edge of society, with little voice and little prestige. But again, for a person of faith, it's the way Abraham lived that's normal: it was all those decades and even centuries of being the establishment that was atypical and even unhealthy. And if the present cultural climate requires us more and more to remember how to live in tents, well, there are some advantages. Think about it. Tents don't require a whole lot of maintenance; the insurance premiums are low; tents are very flexible—you can make them bigger or smaller fairly easily; people who live in tents can move on fairly easily; and (best of all) they're never going to be designated heritage buildings. So for the foreseeable future, the tent is probably a better symbol of the church than the cathedral.

3. BY FAITH, ABRAHAM AND SARAH CONCEIVED A CHILD WHEN THEY WERE TOO OLD TO DO SO (10-12)

The Anglican Church of Canada did a lot of church planting in the 1950s. I've talked to Reg Stackhouse, for instance, who planted St. Matthew's Islington back then. He says it was easy—although going door-to-door is never easy in my experience. But it was literally a case of "If you build it, they will come." After the Second World War, there was a baby boom—not only of human babies, but of baby churches as well.[1]

But that's over sixty years ago. We might ask: Aren't we a bit old to think about having babies? Most denominational leaders have enough worries over shutting down dying churches—without having to listen to some idealistic young church planter with a twinkle in her eye. In other words, we seem to be well past child-bearing age. And yet the Bible is full of unlikely conceptions and births: the unnamed mother of Samson, Hannah, Elizabeth, and of course Mary, and here, Sarah. God seems to specialize in such things. Are our denominations past child-bearing age? Probably. Can our denominations bear children in their old age? Absolutely! Will it be a miracle? Of course! It goes without saying. But that's the name of the game.

---

1. Stackhouse, "Church Planting in the 1950s," 35–41.

4. BY FAITH, ABRAHAM OFFERED UP HIS ONLY SON (17)

Frankly, I find it hard to end with this example because it's such a downer. I'm sure every preacher here has struggled with how to preach this story. I know I have. In this chapter, it's partly that the first three examples Hebrews gives of Abraham's faith are so life-giving: they are pictures of a new journey, a new land, a new baby—full of life and hope. This one speaks bluntly of death and (what looks horribly like) the end of hope. But, from Hebrews' point of view, this last example isn't a downer at all: it comes last because it's the high point of Abraham's faith. The writer of Hebrews is reading the story as a Christian, and through a Christian lens, so he knows that death comes before resurrection, that the death of baptism leads to new life in Christ.

So I don't see any way round saying this: if we are to experience new life in our denominations, we have to be willing for things to die—even if, like Isaac, they don't have to die when it comes to the point. Things that are precious to us, things we thought until recently were essential to being church—just as Abraham thought (and with excellent reason) that his precious Isaac was essential to God's purposes.

We have to ask: What are the Isaacs God might want us to offer? If you are a parish priest or local minister, what are your Isaacs? Perhaps a key layperson who virtually runs the parish, who comes to you in four weeks and says, "I think God wants me to start a fresh expression of church . . ." What if you are a bishop or leader in another denomination? Well, it would be presumptuous for me to make suggestions, but I'm sure you will know what the Isaacs are. What if you are a layperson? Or a theological student? Perhaps your Isaac is a particular vision of what parish ministry ought to look like. And yes, if you're someone who teaches in a seminary, like myself? We have plenty of Isaacs! For all of us, faith means saying, "All things come of thee, and of thine own do we give thee" (1 Chr 29:14). All things: every Isaac we own—or think we own, need, depend on—comes from God, and God may quite soon require them back. We need to have them on an open palm before God—and resist the temptation to close that fist and hang on to them.

So, four examples of Abraham's faith: all of them deeply challenging in our present context. And faith is the key. For the writer to the Hebrews, faith is not, as H. L. Mencken suggested, an "illogical belief in the occurrence of the improbable"[2] or, as Mark Twain thought, "believing what you know ain't

---

2. Mencken, *Mencken Chrestomathy*, 11.

true."[3] No, faith is trusting the character of God and the promises of God. It's just plain old common sense. These things that Hebrews praises in Abraham are not options for the super-spiritual. The whole point is that these are the basics of the life of faith.

But if it sounds like the ultimate challenge (which I suppose it is), Hebrews also offers the ultimate encouragement. So the climax of chapter 11 is really at the beginning of chapter 12. Listen:

> Therefore, since we are surrounded by so great a cloud of witnesses [others who have gone this way of faith before us], let us also lay aside every weight [you know what those weights are in your life as I do in mine] and the sin that clings so closely [most often the comfortable sins nobody notices and that don't get you fired—our desire to be respectable, our desire to be secure, our reluctance to change], and let us run with perseverance the race that is set before us, looking to Jesus the pioneer and perfecter of our faith [this is the way he went], who for the sake of the joy that was set before him endured the cross [the death], disregarding its shame [the loss of dignity, and status, and voice], and has taken his seat at the right hand of the throne of God (12:1–2).

In other words, says Hebrews, don't look in the first place to Abraham but rather look to Jesus—just as Abraham, in a sense, looked to Jesus; he, too, lived this life of risky faith, and by his Spirit he can strengthen us to do it too.

---

3. Twain, *Following the Equator*, 132.

E

Speaking for Myself

WRITERS AND PREACHERS OFTEN have issues to address, problems to analyze, or Bible passages to expound. Readers and listeners always appreciate it when personal insights and experiences are woven into a presentation. Otherwise, they can seem cold and fail to make a connection. But there is such a thing as too much self-revelation. It's one thing for personal stories to be the condiments, adding flavor to the meal, but it's quite another trying to make them the whole meal. Speakers and writers who talk too much and too often about themselves quickly lose their audience.

Here are a few times I have written about personal experience. Sometimes it was because I was asked to do so ("Spirituality in My Sixties"), and sometimes it was simply because, when significant things happen in my life, my instinct is always to want to capture them in words ("Strong and Weak"). But these are the exceptions. I'm not trying to make a meal out of them.

23

Strong and Weak by Andy Crouch[1]

A Personal Case Study

My approach to writing tends to be somewhat cerebral: here's an issue that needs addressing, and I feel I have something to say about it. Many of the pieces in this book are like that. I suppose my attitude to reading is often the same: here's an interesting topic, I wonder what I can learn this time. But occasionally the inspiration is a personal experience which (for those who enjoy writing, anyway) demands to be put on paper. The experience out of which this piece came was vivid enough in itself, but it was given a whole other dimension by what I was reading at the time. What follows was published in the online version of Faith Today, a Canadian Christian magazine, in March/April 2017.

No book is read in a vacuum. You may kid yourself that you are "getting away from it all" to be quiet and simply read, but the "all" never retreats very far. And if the book is any good, it will follow you back into the "all" anyway. And there, the book and your life will find each other and will tangle and fight and perhaps love, and nothing will ever be the same again.

This happened to me recently when I was partway through reading Andy Crouch's newest book, *Strong and Weak*, for a group I belong to.

---

1. Crouch, *Strong and Weak*.

I had been diagnosed with stable angina, which degenerated a few weeks later into unstable angina. I was told to stay home for a week, until the cardiologist could arrange for an angiogram. The angiogram, on a Monday morning, revealed four major blood vessels in trouble, one of them 85% percent blocked, and an appointment was made for quadruple bypass surgery at 9 am two days later.

And then began the wrestling of Crouch's words and my life. At the worst, it was as though his words began to curl off the page and meld into thin, indestructible lines, tying down my life and making me horizontal for the better part of a week. You know the kind of thing: an unbreakable plastic name band, tubes filling my body with various liquids, lines of nylon thread holding edges of flesh together, lines of metal staples like tiny telegraph poles bridging bloody gashes, oxygen tubes poking up my nose, a catheter to drain urine, a heart monitor with five colored wires, and thin blue electrical wires poking out of my chest "just in case." I knew how Gulliver must have felt when the Lilliputians tied him down with their silken cords.

But I need to tell you about the book. Crouch argues that human flourishing—the loving plan of our Creator—consists of two big components, "authority" (by which he means agency, instrumentality, the ability to have significance in the world) and "vulnerability" (the need to be open, to experience love and intimacy, to hurt and be hurt, to forgive and to be forgiven).[2] For each of us, consciously or unconsciously, we seek a healthy blend of those two things.

But things go wrong. We can exaggerate our authority and withdraw our vulnerability. In extreme cases, this produces dictators and oppressors and abusive marriages. And in those circumstances, everyone else's life ecology is thrown off too. When some accumulate authority without vulnerability, more will find they are left with vulnerability but little authority. Flourishing moves out of reach for both groups.

If we plot authority and vulnerability on a two-way axis—which Crouch does—where the vertical represents the direction of authority, and the horizontal is the direction of vulnerability, we have four squares. In the top right, there is maximum flourishing. The top left (authority without vulnerability) and the bottom right (vulnerability but no authority) feed off each other in an unholy synergy. The bottom right, at its simplest of course, is sheer suffering. And the bottom left? No authority, no vulnerability—rich people on a river cruise in Europe!

All this was still fresh in my mind when I showed up at the hospital on that Monday morning.

---

2. Crouch, *Strong and Weak*, 13.

I suspect you know what hospital is like, but as soon as you experience it through Crouch's grid, everything takes on an extra dimension. Think of the hospital hierarchy for a start. The surgeons and doctors are firmly in the top left, the authority square. Some choose to offer a degree of vulnerability, but never much and never for long. It's not their job in this context. Then come the nurses, bearers of needles and compassion, and administrators, the keepers of gates both great and small. The masses of staff—cleaners, bearers of food, wipers of floors, emptiers of garbage, disinfectors of mattresses, launderers—are much closer to the vulnerability line than the authority line: few university degrees here, not many rare skills, little disposable income, and no university policies being written by this group. Thank God for national labor standards and unions.

And so we come to the patients. The story I tell next needs to be a first-person narrative, for obvious reasons, but you may recognize your own experience in it.

I think it is fair to say God has blessed me with a healthy blend of authority and vulnerability. As a result, I generally enjoy a good degree of flourishing in God's world, for which I am grateful. Part of my usual flourishing comes from knowing stuff—Crouch's "authority"—but today the first challenge to my flourishing—apart from the inevitable undercurrent of fear—is that the only knowledge of mine anyone is interested in is what those high in the medical guild have given me to repeat, and the words scratched on the forms I have been given to hand in. Oh, and my date of birth.

And so I enter this world where I feel very small and very scared, and even (though it's not usually dominant) hopeful. I surrender the degree of flourishing God had blessed me with until yesterday, hoping it will only be a temporary sacrifice and I will be back on track soon.

I sit a lot and I wait a lot. I am bored. I read things I have no interest in, out of desperation. I try praying, but it's just words. I have a book (no, not Crouch!) but it's hard to concentrate. Facebook loses its appeal more quickly than usual. I am reminded why we don't watch much TV.

Lots of people with authority bustle around. They have agency in this important world. Their coats and clipboards speak of their authority. This is a place where they have learned to flourish. For them, this world, in some measure or other, gives them a life-giving blend of authority and vulnerability, and it seems to work well for them. Meanwhile, I and others who can do nothing but wait fall slowly away from our normal flourishing and towards that dark, bottom right-hand corner where we will at last be sans everything.

Over the next several hours, I am slowly stripped of those things that make me glad to be alive. I have already canceled lunch with a friend. I have pulled out of a speaking engagement. I explain to my research colleague that she will have to work alone for a bit. I forget the writing projects that I peck away at each day. All the things that make me and my life significant are now on hold. Nobody cares about what I am reading or my grandchildren's art work or what I'm working on. Unlike yesterday, I won't just go and make myself another cup of tea, or see what Amazon has brought to my door. And I certainly won't be updating my Facebook status. The prospect of imminent suffering makes me want to hide and be invisible. I want to be known as flourishing and strong. That's who I really am. I think. Sheer vulnerability without any authority is almost unbearable. It's not the way God has wired us.

The stripping continues. "Put one of these gowns on your back and one on the front, but leave the laces untied. Put your clothes in this plastic bag. Give your watch and your glasses to your wife to take home. Oh, and your wedding ring, of course. You can't take that into surgery. It can get very hot. Then pee into this bottle, put it into that tray over there, and then come and sit in the waiting room." Nobody's being nasty—they're just doing their job—but they're tired and probably bored, like us. Some smile. More sitting, more waiting, more froth on TV.

Of course, I want to be clear: I know I am deliberately allowing these things. No one is to blame for my entry into this frightening world but me. No one forced me. This is not a war forcing me from my home, or a multinational stealing my ancestral lands. I could have said no, and stayed in my familiar world and petted the cat and got the supper together and tried to maintain my flourishing. And, conversely, I know all this impersonal authority swirling around me is ultimately there for my good. Despite appearances, the system is actually benign and pursuing life for me—by way of death.

So, on this day, because an authority figure has said so, I choose to give away the authority that makes me who I am. In its place, I accept vulnerability, and become weak, very weak, as weak as a person can become without actually dying. I no longer grasp at healthy human flourishing, but lay aside all these things. Why? Because I am sick. Without this surrender to suffering, I may die. The only chance of getting my *shalom* back is through this slow stepping down into the cold, dark, alien world Crouch calls "suffering."[3] It's that simple.

It starts small ("Take a number and we'll call you") but wait, it will grow. The stripping goes on. For this surgery, I was shaved (I could not but think of it: "'Let him be shaved!' cried the queen"), then laid flat with my arms outstretched, and strapped to the table. The symbolism was stark—yet I knew deeply what a difference there was, that in my case my captors really did want my good. They wanted to restore my abundance, not stop its flow forever.

The anesthetic was quick and merciful before the knives began their work. Then (I am told) a doctor stopped my heart and lungs, so they could

---

3. Crouch, *Strong and Weak*, 49–72.

not move while they were operated on. Another started the electric saw to sever the breast bone. A third one stripped the little-needed blood vessels from the leg and chest. Sometimes only a knife blade divides this little death from the real thing.

Five hours later, recovery (so-called) begins. Still weak, still suffering, still lacking authority. Things have been taken out of my body and now things are put into my body. The tubes in the throat preventing speech, the catheter up the genitals, chest tubes draining fluid from the chest, blood leaking from under dressings and running down my leg, needing help to get out of bed, to walk, to cough, to pee. More intrusive questions: "Have you passed gas today? Have you had a bowel movement since you woke up?" Nobody asks adults these questions in normal life—only those who have authority over those who suffer.

But slowly, slowly, life begins to return—the difficult climb, inch by inch, out of Crouch's bottom-right quadrant. And at every step, there is grace, usually in small doses—though sometimes I think I couldn't handle it in larger amounts anyway.

A priest friend drives forty minutes to see me, stays five minutes and prays for me, then drives back forty minutes. A male nurse turns out to be a Christian. We have friends in common. He recognizes my "authority" in another context. We become friends. Nurses come at the push of a button, night or day (authority: hah!). I am given a remarkable range of choices of what I would like to eat: more authority. (You won't hear me making jokes about hospital food.) Family come, bringing love and books and cards and music and flowers that help restore my significance. They bring with them the aroma of the flourishing I once knew, and help me have faith it will return.

The surgeon visits daily for a week, sometimes early, sometimes late. Once, she asks, "So, what is it you are a professor of?" She recognizes me as a person who has authority in other contexts. And it's a somewhat vulnerable question to ask: round here, she is the one with the expertise, not me.

One by one, the tubes are removed, the dressings removed, the needles extracted. "This will hurt, but only for a moment. Take a deep breath and hold it. There: it's out!" Each one a liberation. Step by step, my body becomes autonomous again. I put my watch on, my glasses, my wedding ring. Oh joy.

And so the armies of hospital personnel with all their authority do their work. In the course of seven days, my life moved in a matter of a few intense hours from a flourishing top-right quadrant to a deep, dark, bottom-right quadrant—and now it begins to come back again. Slowly the balance of authority and vulnerability is restored to that equilibrium which gives life. But from now on the flourishing will always bear the scars of that time in the darkness. And that too is a good thing.

24

Is "Anglican Evangelical" an Oxymoron?

WYCLIFFE COLLEGE IS "AN *evangelical Anglican*" *college. These days, more than half its students are from evangelical rather than Anglican backgrounds. The college's constitution, however, requires that the Principal be an Anglican clergyman. (The day may well come when the college wants to appoint an Anglican clergywoman, and the constitution will need to change.) The college's worship in the chapel is Anglican. A Lutheran student even said to me once, "Do you know how English the college feels?" (For some reason, I was not aware of it.) Most of the time, however, the blend is comfortable and stimulating.*

In recent years, the terms "evangelical" and "Anglican" have become polarized in popular understanding. It is over-simplifying, but maybe it will suffice to say evangelicals have been painted by the media as right-wing, and Anglicans (as far as they ever attract attention) as left-wing. So it can raise eyebrows to call yourself "an evangelical Anglican."

In view of this, twice in my time at the college, The Morning Star *has run a series of editorials by faculty on the subject "What is an Evangelical Anglican?" The following was my contribution, first in November 2003 and then again (with some tweaks) in March of 2013. I realize belatedly that my approach is modeled on that of John Stott's 1986 article, "I Believe in the Church of England."*

G. K. Chesterton is supposed to have once contributed to a correspondence in *The Times* newspaper of London about what is wrong with the world. Chesterton's letter ended the correspondence, since there really was no way to follow it. He wrote, "What is wrong with the world? I am. Yours sincerely, G. K. Chesterton."[1] By analogy, when I am asked, "Can someone be an Anglican Evangelical? Isn't it an oxymoron?" I am tempted to reply, "Well, I am."

So, at the risk of seeming self-indulgent, let me tell you what this means to me. It means I consider myself a Christian first of all, an evangelical Christian second, and an Anglican evangelical Christian third. They are like three concentric circles, Christian being the biggest, and Anglican evangelical the smallest.

To begin with the first, when I say I am a Christian, I mean I believe Jesus Christ is Lord of the universe, Savior of the world, and Head of the church, and that I have given my life, heart and soul and mind and strength to him. My heart's desire is to see him more clearly, love him more dearly, and follow him more nearly, day by day. (I think this is what you call wearing your heart on your sleeve, something Anglicans don't do a whole lot. So be it. I was recently reading Augustine's *Confessions*, so that might explain it.)

Being first and foremost a Christian also means I feel solidarity with a Pentecostal in Argentina, a Quaker in Kenya, a member of the Brethren in Spain, a Catholic from India, and a member of an underground house church in China. Other differences, national and linguistic as well as denominational, pale into insignificance in the light of our common allegiance to Jesus Christ. If I were primarily an Anglican, such fellowship would be much harder to come by.

When I say, secondly, I am an evangelical, I mean I belong to that part of the Christian community which emphasizes the importance of the Bible as the primary source of the church's authority, and the gospel as the source of the church's vitality. There are other hallmarks of evangelicalism, but I would argue that all others are secondary to these. As John Stott (that uncrowned Pope of Anglican evangelicalism in the twentieth century) says, "Evangelicals are Bible people, and they are Gospel people."[2] To me, these two convictions are as central to authentic Christianity as the Trinity and the mandate to love my neighbor.

I suppose if the whole church decided tomorrow that the Bible and the gospel were as important as evangelicals believe, then the term "evangelical" wouldn't be needed anymore, and I for one would not miss it. Until then, I

---

1. The story may be apocryphal. The Chesterton Society discusses the question here: https://www.chesterton.org/wrong-with-world.

2. Stott, *What is an Evangelical?*, 3–4.

am content to be called an evangelical, not as a member of a party (heaven forbid) but because of those convictions about the Bible and the gospel.

And, thirdly, when I say I am an Anglican, I guess I am saying that, among all the denominational tribes in the world, this one is my home, my family. As for why I am an Anglican, I would say I appreciate a number of things:

- For a start, I am glad to be part of a tradition which has a strong sense of history. For many other evangelicals, not much happened between the end of Acts and Luther nailing his ninety-five theses to the Wittenberg church door in 1517.

- I also find here a sense of intellectual and spiritual freedom within broad Christian boundaries. I think of one friend who has not been allowed to join the evangelical church she has attended and served for twenty years because she cannot endorse their official statement on eschatology. There will always be issues worth disagreeing over in the family, of course, even passionately, but not as many as for some evangelical churches.

- Then there is the liturgy, which links me with other churches around the world and through the centuries, and is not dependent on an individual minister's whim, mood, vocabulary, or spirituality.

- Finally, I value the episcopate, particularly when bishops lead and teach us in godly ways. I have known independent churches (a phrase that is itself an oxymoron) that get into trouble and have no idea what to do because they have no outside authority to intervene.

This is not to say that I have always attended Anglican churches. Certainly, I was raised Anglican (in the Church in Wales, not to be confused with the Church of England).[3] But I have also been an attender/adherent/member of a Baptist church, a Plymouth Brethren assembly, a charismatic Anglican church (which was not always recognizable as Anglican), a Presbyterian church, and (presently) a church one long-term member described to me as "Anglo-Catholic in process of evangelicalization." It has always depended on the context, though St. John's is officially our parish church. And I have attended churches of many more traditions, from Vineyard to Alliance to Roman Catholic.

For me, returning to the Anglican Church almost forty years ago had a sense about it of coming home, having tried other options and found them, for various reasons, lacking. And on the days when I wonder why I stay

---

3. Rowan Williams, who was Archbishop of Canterbury from 2002 till 2012, was previously Archbishop of Wales, thus becoming the first Archbishop of Canterbury to be appointed from outside England for centuries.

(and there have been a few of those), part of my answer is, "To whom shall we go?" Not that the Anglican Church has "the words of life" but there are those other things I appreciate, and, when combined with the words of life, to me it's irresistible.

So I am Christian first, evangelical second, and Anglican third. Could I give them up? Well, I could probably live without the Anglican Church, sad though it would be. If there were only a Baptist church in my town, and the nearest Anglican church was half-an-hour's drive away, I would commit myself to the Baptist church, but sneak away (hopefully with the pastor's blessing) to the Anglican church from time to time.

Could I be other than evangelical? That's tougher, because so much of my understanding of Christian faith is through that lens. But could I give up being a Christian? Like the disciples of old, I would have to reply, "Lord, to whom shall we go? You have the words of eternal life" (John 6:68).

25

Spirituality in My Sixties

MY FRIEND MATT IS *a church planter. But I met Matt before he ever planted a church, when he was an Associate Pastor at Grindstone Community Church in Waterdown, Ontario. I did a couple of workshops there on evangelism, which is my usual schtick, but then he asked me to do something quite different, something I had never been asked to do before. The church was doing a sermon series on spirituality in the decades of life, from the teens on up, and they asked me to contribute one on "Spirituality in My Sixties." I thought this was a great idea, and what follows is the sermon I preached on that topic, in March of 2014.*

My text is from Isaiah 43. I would have included it in the "Signature Sermons" section, because this has been one of the most generative texts in my life for the past forty years, and I have preached on it in many contexts. However, I thought it fit better under "Personal Statements," for reasons that will be obvious.

I need to add one footnote. As I was leaving after the service, I asked Matt who was preaching the following week, because I would quite like to hear about spirituality in one's seventies.

"Oh, nobody," he answered, "this is the end of the series."

SPIRITUALITY IN MY SIXTIES   137

The average lifespan of someone in Canada today is around eighty years. Suppose eighty years is represented by a single day running from 7 am to 11 pm.

That means one hour represents five years, so a decade is represented by two hours: ages one to ten would then be from 7 till 9 am; from ten to twenty, 9 till 11 am; your twenties, 11 till 1 pm; thirties, 1 till 3 pm—and so on through the day, until you get to the sixties, which would be represented by 7 till 9 pm; and seventy to eighty, 9 till 11 pm. So if I'm presently sixty-seven, I am at 8:36 pm. But who's counting?

This is the age at which a number of old jokes come true.

- Conversations with peers become organ recitals.
- Getting older isn't great but it's better than the alternative.
- Pretty girls smile at you, then tell you that you remind them of . . . their grandfather.

So in this process of getting older, what difference does it make if you are in your sixties and a follower of Jesus?

Gideon Bibles have a helpful index, enabling you to look up relevant passages of Scripture for the crises of life: "If depressed . . . If faced with a decision . . . If in need of strength . . ." But there is no single passage of the Bible marked, "If in your sixties, look here"—not that being in your sixties is a crisis. Of course. Even if it is 8:36 pm.

There are some age-specific Scriptures. Perhaps the most famous is Psalm 90:10 (KJV):

> The days of our years are threescore years and ten; and if by reason of strength they be fourscore years, yet is their strength labour and sorrow; for it is soon cut off, and we fly away.

It somehow seems more sonorous in the King James Version. But it seems like little more than a reminder that "A lot of people get to nine o'clock, but not so many to eleven." Thanks a lot. I knew that already.

My experience is more that familiar Scriptures take on new significance at different stages of life. There is one passage in particular that has been significant in my life for at least thirty-five years. It is Isaiah 43:16–21, and it speaks to the past, present, and future of the universe and of our lives.

The time is towards the end of Judah's seventy years' exile in Babylon, roughly around 500 BCE. Isaiah's words are intended as an encouragement to the people: they will soon be free, and then it will be time for them to return to Jerusalem, to rebuild the city and the temple, and to start a new life. But not all of them are interested. Let's start with what Isaiah says about:

1. THE PAST: "FORGET THE FORMER THINGS, OR CONSIDER THE THINGS OF OLD."

Frankly, that's easy to say, not so easy to do. One thing people do in later life is to evaluate the past, both the good and the bad, and try to make sense of it. Did I make good choices? Did I invest my life wisely? It's difficult to know how to measure.

I once did a debate with a philosophy professor about the existence of God in front of 1,000 students at McGill University. How does that rate on God's scale? That was pretty good, surely? Not many people have that kind of thing on their CV. But then, was that more or less valuable than spending an hour having a cup of tea with a lonely old lady? We know perfectly well that that's a trick question, so we immediately say the old lady—but what if I did it hoping she would put me in her will? (Actually, she did.) And which required the more preparation, effort, and adrenaline? You can guess.

So it's not clear how you measure these things. Even Paul can say: "My conscience is clear [meaning, I think I've done OK], but that does not make me innocent [meaning, my own judgment isn't good enough]. It is the Lord who judges me" (1 Cor 4:4).

So is there anything we can do to measure the past, except leave it to the kindness and justice of God? There is one insight I have found helpful. I look back on the many years I spent working with university students, not in big events, but usually in small groups and one on one. What happened to those students? Are they still growing in their discipleship all these years later? Did I help? A number I know about—sometimes the answer is good news, sometimes not—but most I don't. We have lost touch.

So I find myself asking, "Did I waste my time? Did I do things wrong? Could I have done better?" In the end, I decided the only thing I could say in all honesty was I tried to love them. Was it pure love? Of course not. Working with them was my job, it gave me pleasure, and they liked me (and we all like to be liked). I got a lot out of it. But did I love them? I did try.

What about failures? Sure, there were failures. Regrets? Absolutely. Things I would do differently another time? Of course. Once, Jane, a staff member I was trying to supervise, had a dramatic burnout and had to leave staff. Did I feel bad? What do you think?

Édith Piaf is famous for the song, "Non, je ne regrette rien." It's a wonderful and dramatic song, but the sentiment is frankly ridiculous. How can anyone say they don't regret a thing? How can that be an ideal for anyone to strive for or boast about? What about the people we (and without doubt, Édith Piaf too) have hurt, for a start? How can we not regret certain things?

Well maybe, if you don't know grace, that's the only way you can live with yourself and your memories.

But grace means you can say, "Yes, I blew it." Of course, there are regrets. Grace also means you don't need to linger over your failures. There's no need to play them and replay them over and over in your head, when God has forgiven you and moved on. In fact, to dwell on them can be simple pride. Failures? Yes. But thank God for grace, and move on with God.

Now, you may be saying, "Isn't this verse about forgetting the past? But here you are remembering it." Guilty as charged. I told you it was difficult.

But actually, Isaiah 43 is not saying forget everything; rather, it is saying, "Remember the right things, and remember in the right way." I say that because there's an odd thing right here at the beginning of the reading. Just before the bit about forgetting, the passage reads:

> Thus says the Lord, who makes a way in the sea, a path in the mighty waters, who brings out chariot and horse, army and warrior; they lie down, they cannot rise, they are extinguished, quenched like a wick (16–17).

Why is that odd? Because it looks remarkably as if God is reminding them of something, specifically of the exodus! I want to ask, "Lord, if they're to forget, why exactly are you reminding them?"

The only answer I can think of is they are remembering the wrong things. Maybe they are recalling good times in Babylon. Some (think about Daniel) had done well in Babylon. Their children had grown up and got married and had children there. Seventy years was a long time. There was a whole new generation who had not known Jerusalem and the land firsthand. So remembering those things might well make them reluctant to leave.

Or maybe the older generation in particular was remembering bad things. Before they left Judah, friends and family had been killed, the temple had been destroyed, and they had left Jerusalem in ruins. It would be a nightmare to go back! (You can follow the story of how Judah responded to Isaiah in the books of Ezra and Nehemiah.)

It seems as though remembering good things and remembering bad things can equally hold us back from following God. Memories can be a ball and chain, keeping us from moving forward.

But if they remembered the right things—things God had done, like the exodus—instead of being a ball and chain, memory could have been a springboard into following God in the present.

When I remember the story of Jane, I could just remember my failure. But there's another story: it turned out both of us were in the wrong jobs.

She went on to become a very effective psychotherapist; and I moved out of staff supervision and went on to do student evangelism full-time.

That was the work of God—a new thing.

How does it affect me to remember those things? If I only remembered my failures, it might hold me back. But when I remember what God has done in the past, remembering can actually encourage me to trust God for the future. So let's turn to thinking about:

2. THE FUTURE: "I WILL MAKE A WAY IN THE WILDERNESS AND RIVERS IN THE DESERT."

If it's 8:36, time is running out, and it's getting late.

Not surprisingly, I find I think about death more frequently and more seriously. A twinge in my left arm and I assume it's a heart attack. A spot on my back, and I assume it's cancer. I don't think I'm alone. I can't find the origin of the quote, "No human being can look their own mortality in the face without flinching." (Maybe it's too obvious to have a single source.) Christians are no exception to his rule, and we should not expect to be.

You may know that Will Ferrell movie, *Stranger than Fiction* (not your typical Will Ferrell movie). It is a great study of predestination and freewill, and how a creature relates to their creator. Will Ferrell plays an accountant who discovers his life is being dictated by someone else. That someone turns out to be a novelist (played by Emma Thompson), who is writing the story of his life. If that's not confusing enough, he discovers that in her novels, the hero always dies. When he discovers this, he comes out with the poignant line: "I can't die right now. This is really bad timing."[1]

Well, that's true for most of us. Whatever the time is, it will in many cases seem like really bad timing. Jack, my spiritual director, once said, "We will all die unfinished—with appointments in our diaries, emails unanswered, things we meant to do, things we meant to say."

For most of us, there will never come a day when we say, "Well, there we are. I'm all done. Nothing in my diary, updated my Facebook status, email inbox is empty. The only thing left in my diary for today is dying. Guess I better get on with it."

It takes courage to prepare for death. My wife and I have made some of the preparations: we made our will (not too difficult); made notes for our funeral services (that was almost fun); and chosen a grave plot and paid for it (that was a challenge). You may know the story about the woman who gave her husband a grave plot for his birthday. The following year she gave

---

1. Forster, *Stranger than Fiction*, 1:27:00–1:27:07.

him nothing. When he asked why, she said, "You haven't used the gift I gave you last year yet." Well, we haven't used our grave plots yet, either. Have we talked to a funeral director about caskets? Not quite.

This is where Isaiah's words are so helpful. At the heart of his message is the statement, "Behold, I am doing a new thing" (19). Creating new things is not something God did on this one occasion and never again. In fact, the idea of God doing new things resonates through the whole of Scripture from the start to the finish. The Bible begins with, "In the beginning, God created . . ." and ends, "I saw a new heaven and a new earth," and there are lots more examples in between—a new covenant, a new commandment, and a new birth, for a start.

And of course, in the very middle is the best, biggest, brightest of God's new things: Jesus Christ—his life, death, and resurrection. That new thing is what shines its light on the end of the journey, and on everything on the path between here and there. Listen to what Isaiah says about the journey:

> I will make a way in the wilderness and rivers in the desert. The wild animals will honor me, the jackals and the ostriches; for I give water in the wilderness, rivers in the desert, to give drink to my chosen people, the people whom I formed for myself so that they might declare my praise (19–21).

Isaiah knows that God's new things are not necessarily easy—they may be challenging, they may feel like a desert. Indeed, the route from Babylon to Jerusalem involved crossing hundreds of miles of desert. God does not remove the challenge, but says instead, "I will provide you with the resources you need—a way in the wilderness and rivers in the desert—so you can keep going till you arrive at your destination." And that goal—for the exiles—was Jerusalem; for us—the new Jerusalem.

So in those moments when I worry about death, I find it helpful to say to myself, "In life and in death I belong to Jesus Christ." For a time, I didn't know where I picked this up, so I looked it up. It is right at the beginning of the Heidelberg Catechism, written in 1563, one of the great founding documents of the Protestant Reformation, and still used in Christian Reformed churches. Let me read it:

> Q. 1. What is your only comfort, in life and in death?
> A. That I belong—body and soul, in life and in death—not to myself but to my faithful Savior, Jesus Christ, who at the cost of his own blood has fully paid for all my sins and has completely freed me from the dominion of the devil; that he protects me so well that without my Father in heaven not a hair can fall from my head; indeed, that everything must fit his purpose for my

salvation. Therefore, by his Holy Spirit, he also assures me of eternal life, and makes me wholeheartedly willing and ready from now on to live for him.

For a follower of Jesus, that's the only sensible way to face the future: "In life and in death I belong to Jesus Christ." I recommend saying it to yourself in moments of darkness and fear and doubt. It's what I have been learning to do. But Isaiah has one more thing to say, this time about:

3. THE PRESENT: "BEHOLD, I AM DOING A NEW THING. NOW IT SPRINGS FORTH: DO YOU NOT PERCEIVE IT?"

Why is God so concerned to do new things? The answer is simple. It's certainly not that God likes novelty for its own sake. God does new things for two reasons: (a) God is love, and (b) the world is full of sin and evil and suffering. You put those two things together, and it is pretty obvious this kind God is going to be doing new things until all that is changed, and all things are made new.

But Isaiah asks, "Do you not perceive it?" One thing that happens as we get older is we can get lazy, or complacent, or overly introspective. "I've done enough, I'm tired, it's someone else's turn." That attitude can prevent us noticing the new things God is doing. Hence these words, "Do you not perceive it?"

What new things is God doing these days? I am excited about some very positive things in the life of the church: the growth of the church in the Global South; lots of new adventures in church planting; Christians engaging with the post-Christendom world with boldness and creativity; Christians participating in the environmental movement and the movement for racial justice; some of the amazing younger leaders God is raising up, even here in our own city. And that's just for starters.

Those are positive things. But some new things are more difficult, particularly on a personal level. I find I don't get over things so quickly; health matters that would have resolved easily twenty years ago now hang on; I have less energy than I used to. Sometimes, I see others take my ideas and take them in new directions I don't especially appreciate.

But then I realize: that's right. God never said his new things would necessarily be easy. In order to embrace the new thing, we often have to give up the old thing. When I complain, I find the Lord is not terribly sympathetic. "Um, do you not remember I told you that you had to die in order to live? Get used to it. These are just rehearsals."

Ignatius Loyola founded the Jesuits, the Roman Catholic missionary order, in the 1500s. The Jesuits were always edgy and regarded with some suspicion by the Roman Catholic hierarchy. Once someone asked Loyola, "If the pope shut down the Jesuits, what would you do?"

He thought for a moment, then said, "I would pray about it for fifteen minutes and then it would be OK."[2]

That's how much he was able to keep his life's work in an open palm before God. I confess I'm not there yet.

How do we learn to let go? One way, I think, is to learn that none of this is about us—our projects, our interests, our reputation, our wisdom. It's about the gospel. And one of the new things God has been doing in my life in recent years is giving me a bigger appreciation of what the gospel is: not just forgiveness of sins—though it is that, thank God; not just a relationship with God—though we would be nothing without it; not just about life after death—praise God for that! But the gospel is about God making all things new—God through Christ renewing not just us but the whole cosmos. As Ephesians puts it, the gospel is "a plan for the fullness of time, to gather up all things in [Christ], things in heaven and things on earth" (Eph 1:10).

That puts past, future, and present into perspective: my life, my death, your life, your death, all we are, all we have, all we do, everything we love, everyone we love—all those things only come together and make sense in light of God's amazing plan.

What is the heart of Christian faith? I like to put it this way: our loving Creator wants this world to be filled with joy. Yet every day you and I mess that up. And God, through Jesus, says, "You can start over. Stop what you're doing, follow me, and little by little I will restore joy to you—and through you I will begin to restore joy to the world."

On one level it makes no difference which decade of life we are in. God's invitation—and God's challenge—is always to follow Jesus, so God can restore joy in us—in spite of suffering, beyond suffering—and through us to the whole world.

---

2. This is probably apocryphal. However, see https://saltandlighttv.org/blogfeed/getpost.php?id=50062.

26

The Christmas Gift I Never Asked for or Expected

This piece needs no introduction, except to say it was my editorial in The Morning Star *in January 2004.*

If there's one thing worse than getting irritated at Christmas, it's getting irritated about Christmas. Then that, of course, produces guilt ("Irritated about Christmas? But I thought you were religious!"), which is also very irritating. You know what I mean? OK, I confess, this is not just theory: I was the one who was irritated. As if you hadn't guessed.

What was it that bugged me so much? More confession: well-meaning friends, whose letters and cards urged me to "take time this Christmas season to meditate on the real meaning of Christmas." Sure, sure. Reflect. That takes time, you know. When do I have time around Christmas to "reflect?" Get real. What planet are these people from? Do they really think I am going to have a leisurely hour when I go into the den by myself, Bible in hand, and meditate in deep silence on "the real meaning of Christmas"? Give me a break. Even supposing I could find the time, do you think it's just going to happen like that? I can't manufacture a revelation quite so readily. "Eureka! Eureka! I've just discovered the true meaning of Christmas!" Somehow I knew it wouldn't work. That then brought on a new feeling: spiritual inadequacy. (Since I knew it was a silly feeling, I simply found it irritating, and that certainly didn't help.) But I had reckoned without God. Always a dangerous thing to do.

For reasons I won't bore you with, I ended up going to church three times between 7pm on Christmas Eve and noon on Christmas Day, and to three different churches at that. And three different things happened, each calling for Kleenex. I suppose you could call them epiphanies, really, except they weren't.

The first service was the Christmas Eve family service at my own parish church, St. John the Evangelist in Hamilton. It was a glorious service, but it was during the prayers of the people that Thing #1 happened. Susan was praying, and in her prayers she prayed for those who were parents—a nice idea, since Mary and Joseph became parents at Christmas. We prayed for those who were becoming parents this Christmas, and for those being born this Christmas. That was nice too. But then she led us in prayer for those who were losing parents this Christmas. Then we prayed for those parents who were dying this Christmas. I thought of two fathers I knew of who had already died this Christmastime. And of my grandmother, who lived with us and who died on Christmas Eve when I was eleven. Yes, of course: the joy of Christmas does not mean pretending that suffering and death don't exist. God knows those things too. Kleenex time.

Then, at 11pm, we were at Trinity, Streetsville, where Harold Percy was the rector at the time. During the service there was a dramatic sketch where two of Harold's sons, Joel and Benjamin, acted an older angel explaining to a younger angel just what God had done for that "little dim planet down there" at Christmas time. The younger one was horrified.

"You mean he changed into . . . something else?" [Herion asked].

"He became very small," replied Raphael. "Nothing more than a seed—and was born onto the earth."

"How horrible," Herion exclaimed. "It's a wonder to me that he didn't come to grief down there on that miserable place."

"Well," said Raphael slowly. "He did . . . and he didn't."[1]

There it was: Thing #2. The story came afresh through the ears of Herion, who had never heard it before, and it moved me.

Finally, on Christmas morning, we went to a Christian Reformed church where we have a number of friends. A young woman got up to do the New Testament reading, and it happened to be Philippians 2. Little did I know that Thing #3 was imminent. I merely thought, "What a good idea.

---

1. Burbridge and Watts, *Lightning Sketches*, 28–31.

Makes a change from the Christmas story," and began to follow in my head, as the familiar words came out: "though he was in the form of God, he did not regard equality with God as something to be exploited . . ." Then my whole nervous system went on red alert: without looking, I had caught a different tone to the reading. I looked up. I was right: the woman was crying as she read. She hesitated for a second, but then continued, her tears continuing, to the end of the passage: "that Jesus Christ is Lord, to the glory of God the Father." Weeping? At a familiar Bible passage? Yes, of course. She had understood what she was reading. This was not just words, this was reality. She had realized what I had not—the incredible import of what she was reading. "Emptied himself." "Obedient to the point of death." "God highly exalted him." Yes, yes, that's it, that's it. And for the third time in sixteen hours, tears came to my eyes.

I suppose I should have known. After all, "They shall name him Emmanuel, which means 'God is with us'" (Matt 1:23). Jesus was Emmanuel for me that Christmastime. Jesus is "God with us," every day of the year that was past and of the year that was to come. And he always will be Emmanuel, God with us, forever. Maybe we will know Jesus with us when we least expect it. It's wise to keep some Kleenex on hand. You never know.

27

How (Not) to Ask for Money

True Confessions of a Fundraiser

THE PETER PRINCIPLE IS *not as well known today as it was in the 1970s, but it is still useful to know about. It states that people in a hierarchy are promoted "to the level of their incompetence."*[1] *This began to apply in my life in 1982, when I was made Area Director of IVCF in the Eastern Ontario area. The job included at least two things I was not very good at—staff supervision and fundraising. In the 1990s, I moved into a ministry of evangelistic speaking in the universities, which was a much better match for my gifts, and I never looked back.*

This piece is a reflection from that time when I was a director, and gives you a sense of why I was never at ease in the role. This was published in Christian Week, *an interdenominational Canadian newspaper, around 1990. I think it still raises some good questions.*

I do not look forward to the Christmas mail for two reasons. Partly I dread the endless cries for financial help. From about December 1st onward, they stagger through the mailbox, wounded and pitiful, ten at a time, headed straight for my heart. And my checkbook. Would I please, please, please help the orphans, those without Bibles, those with heart disease, those

---

1. Peter and Hull, *Peter Principle*, 25.

serving the poor, those with kidney problems, the lepers, artists with disabilities, and so on? Every mail delivery brings a new set of needs.

Many of the appeals have a tried-and-true formula that you and I know well by now: (a) our organization is making superhuman progress in the face of great difficulties; (b) unfortunately, there is a serious financial need that threatens our whole program; (c) the entire future of our organization depends on you; (d) if everyone who receives this letter gave $X (or $XX, or even $XXX), everything would be fine, the work would go forward again, and you would know our eternal gratitude. Eternal, at least, until the next appeal. Oh yes, and then (e) the PS: Do it now: we are depending on you!!! (The number of exclamation marks may vary.)

I oscillate between guilt ("Maybe I should sell the car and give them the proceeds"), frustration ("I'm not even going to open this lot") and incredulity ("These all have the same crisis—on December 1st?"). I hate it. I get mad at myself for not knowing what to do. And I detest the system where people feel they have to do this. Merry Christmas indeed.

The other reason I dread the Christmas mail is related but rather different: I have to write one of these financial appeals. Why? Because I work for a parachurch organization that has no source of income except that which people choose to donate. And the fact is many people donate only when asked to do so—especially when asked at Christmas. Our income in December (like that of other charities) is far higher than in any other month of the year. So I have to write—right?

Maybe I should refuse to write it, and avoid the Christmas begging-letter rat-race altogether. The problem is, my staff and their families—not to mention my own family—depend on those big donations in December. So what can I do? Write in November, before people are feeling particularly generous? In January, when the rush is over but no one has money left to give? No, December is it. That's when people are in the mood to give, apparently.

When I sit down to write my letter, there is no shortage of expert advice at hand. Researchers have tabulated our responses to various appeals—it's called the science of direct mail—and they know what will persuade us to give.

- "Write on one side of the paper only" used to be a good rule (people don't want to read a book about your financial needs); now two sides are found to be more "effective." (For "effective," read: "produces more money.")
- Tell them how well you're doing (no one wants to back a loser).
- Start off with a story (catch their interest).

- Make the paragraphs short (easier to skim that way).
- Suggest serious need ("we need your help") but not panic ("we are virtually bankrupt").
- Suggest how much people should give (most people will in fact give one of the amounts you suggest).
- Finally, add a PS: people remember that last line.

I don't know about you, but I hate reading letters written on that model. I know perfectly well what's going on, and I feel used. Manipulated. Certainly not inclined to give. But for me, there is the added problem: I simply don't want to write a letter like that. Do I have an option? I will not play games with people, and yet I do need to write a Christmas appeal letter.

I have a radical idea: maybe I will try being straightforward.

For instance, I could make it clear from the first sentence that this is a financial appeal. Then people won't feel sucked in because I tried to hide that fact until halfway through. I may tell a story to illustrate what God is doing through my organization, but it will be a typical story, not an extraordinary one. I will not play on people's emotions. I will not underline, especially in color. I will state how much money we need before the year-end (or whenever) without drama or exaggeration. And there will be no PS.

At the same time, I have to confess, something inside me still wants to ask: Will it work? Will honesty pay the bills? My answer is yes—at least sometimes. When I have tried to write Christmas letters on the straightforward model, there has generally been a wonderful response. The most amazing year was probably the one when I wrote about the problem of how to decide which charities to support at Christmas, and encouraged people to support Power to Change (another student ministry), the Salvation Army, and the Heart Foundation—oh, and maybe InterVarsity as well, if there was anything left over. I learned something that year, a new meaning to laying down your life in order to find life.

Does that mean honesty always pays? Certainly not. No one ever guaranteed it would—at least in this life. More than one fundraiser, determined to be truthful, has found (for instance) that if you tell people your income is on target, they will stop giving. The only advantage then, as far as I can see, is that your next appeal letter can describe the financial emergency with perfect honesty.

So does that mean I can be honest if it induces people to give, but if not, not? Already, my heart warns me I am in danger of writing cleverly "honest," even "naïve," letters, not because I think it's important to be honest, but because they are "effective" (see definition above). My "honesty" can easily become as manipulative as someone else's proven marketing technique.

I believe there is a more fundamental question here. Better letters are not really the answer. Indeed, the answer does not lie with the letter-writer at all, but with the donor. After all, the only reason the marketing people have data to work with ("Only 18.3 percent of your mailing list responded to your latest appeal") is because we do in fact support organizations when they make an appeal we like. We the donors have allowed them to exploit our weaknesses because we do not guard against our weaknesses. If I say "Yes" to the free book offer (with donations of $50 or more), then I can expect to get more free book offers. In other words, if I reward the attempt to manipulate me, then I am encouraging the manipulator to try again. It's as simple as that.

Our best defense is to be more thoughtful about our giving. I need to research the organizations I am thinking of supporting. Do I have personal reason to be grateful to them? Do they do what they claim to do? What do the people on the receiving end of their work say—to me, not to the organization? What do I know of their staff and their track record in ministry? Are they financially accountable? Do I know (or know of) the people on their board of trustees? When I know the answers to these questions, I am not as vulnerable to a clever selling job in the mail.

After that, I need to commit myself to supporting those organizations I do like on a regular basis. Then they won't need to send me panic letters (sorry, "urgent need" letters) every few months, because their income will be steady month by month. Simple, really.

Of course, that takes time and work. But it's a choice. Either we as donors take on that kind of responsibility, or we may expect more stereotyped appeal letters from the PR people. The responsible approach is better in the long run, not only for us as donors, but also for the organizations themselves. Ultimately, it is a kindness to throw the manipulative letters in the garbage. Or, better, send them back, explaining why. I've done that. Show them we're not fooled, that we don't respond to emotional blackmail and tempting free gifts. (If you get a letter from me that you don't like, let me know.) Like you, I want to be treated like the thoughtful, intelligent, Christian adult I would like to be one day.

So as I, and hundreds like me, write our financial appeals this December, pray for us, that we will write with integrity and honesty and humor. That the science of direct mail will become a dead art. And, particularly, that in the long run (may it be a short run) the needs of all worthwhile organizations will be met in better ways. Then, maybe, secular organizations will want to follow our model of fundraising, instead of us following theirs. Now that would make for a memorable Christmas.

F

Redeeming Doctrine

FOR MANY PEOPLE, DOCTRINE seems dry and boring. We use the example of debating how many angels can dance on the head of a pin, because it seems to us an example of the ridiculousness of doctrine. On the other hand, if you have read C. S. Lewis's cosmic trilogy, you will appreciate why the nature of angels, and how much space they take up, can actually be a very interesting topic.

I have come to appreciate doctrine—which literally means no more than teaching—as the physiology of the Christian faith. You can be a perfectly good first-aider without a detailed knowledge of anatomy (though I certainly hope you know some), but if you are a doctor or a surgeon, you had better know every detail of the human body.

Usually doctrine is implicitly woven into the writing and speaking of Christian teachers, whether we are aware of it or not, but here are a few occasions when I have been asked—or have chosen—to address specific doctrines directly.

28

Why Arius was Wrong

THE ANGLICAN DIOCESE OF Niagara has for years prided itself on being in the vanguard of social movements like that for same-sex equality. The editor of our diocesan newspaper, Chris Grabiec, was a friend, even though we differed on a number of important issues, and he graciously published a number of my articles, including several that represented a more traditional view than his own.

In June 2008, he wrote an editorial called, "Time for a Christian Truce," where he suggested that all the major divisions in the history of the church (including the Protestant Reformation) were over secondary issues, and that Christians should stick together, whatever they believe. One of his examples concerned the argument over the nature of Christ (how much human? how much divine?). After all, he wrote, "Let's be honest for a moment. Who knows who was right in the Christological arguments of the third century? We know who won, but who really knows who was right?"[1] The bait was simply too tempting. Chris graciously published my rejoinder in September 2008.

Like all good editors, Chris Grabiec loves controversy, and, if necessary, will stir the pot himself. So, not wanting to disappoint him, I want to respond

---

1. Grabiec, "Time for a Christian Truce," 1.

to his innocent-sounding but deliberately provocative question about the Arian controversy of the fourth century, "Who knows who was right?"

Let's be clear first of all what the controversy was all about. Arius (ca. 250–336 CE) argued that Christ was a created being, although the most important of God's creations. While he was the agent of the rest of creation, Christ should certainly not be thought of as God. Athanasius (ca. 296–373 CE), in reply, argued the view that, historically, won the day—that Christ was in fact fully God, not created but eternally begotten.

What a yawn! Who cares what obscure male theologians split hairs about 1,600 years ago? Athanasius's victory is enshrined in the Nicene Creed, with its mysterious phrases, saying Jesus was "God from God, light from light, very God from very God." As Bishop Bothwell wrote in *The Niagara Anglican* back in May 2005, "who the heck knows what [that] really means?"[2] And, for goodness sake, what does it matter whether Jesus was God anyway? My guess is that most Anglicans have grave doubts about it. As Chris said in his editorial, issues like the ordination of women or the blessing of same-sex unions seem much more relevant to life today.

I believe, however, that Athanasius was right and Arius was wrong, and that the church's choice to follow Athanasius was absolutely crucial for the future. It has affected such crucial areas as how we view God, human nature, and salvation. Historically, this choice led to a new value being placed on the lives of children and (according to René Girard) to the idea of the hospital as a place where anybody could get help. In the long run, Athanasius's view even plays into how we view women's ordination and same sex blessings. If we had followed Arius, the world would be a very different place.

So, for example, if Jesus is God incarnate, he gives us insights into God that we will not find anywhere else. We can look at his compassion for the hurting and marginalized, or his impatience with religious hypocrisy, and say, "Wow! So God is like that!" Arius thought God was fundamentally unknowable, so no incarnation which could make God knowable was even possible. Athanasius, on the other hand, said (in effect), "Yes, God is beyond our knowing, and yet God has made himself known to us uniquely in the God-man Jesus.

So here is our first challenge: Is Jesus God making God's own self known to us? Or do we have to remain agnostic, with your guess as to what God is like being as good as mine? You can choose agnosticism, of course, if you think the evidence supports it. But what has driven the church over the centuries, and given it joy and energy for its work, is the conviction that Jesus was (in some mysterious sense) God incarnate.

2. Grabiec, "Time for a Christian Truce," 6.

Secondly, if Jesus is God incarnate, that gives immense dignity to human beings. It means that, in spite of our folly and sin, God still thought sufficiently highly of the human race to become one of us. God loved the world that much. If Arius was right, on the other hand, God did not actually stoop to become a human being. The unknowable God simply sent another of God's creatures to this world. Nice, but hardly the same thing.

One of Athanasius's main arguments against Arius concerned salvation. Human beings were in such a mess, he argued, that they could not be saved by another human being, even a supernaturally created being. Only God the Creator had the power to sort us out. Athanasius would agree with Paul: "God was in Christ, reconciling the world unto himself" (2 Cor 5:19 KJV).

Whether you buy that piece of the argument depends, of course, on how bad you think the human situation was before Christ came. Did we really need "redemption from sin" (whatever those words might mean)? If not, then you don't need an incarnation. It depends, too, on why you think Jesus came. If he came to offer us roughly the same good moral advice as other religious teachers, then—sure—he doesn't have to be God to do that. It also depends on what you think was happening on the cross. If it was merely the sad but inevitable end to the career of a man who challenged the status quo too much, then that has nothing to do with salvation. In fact, it's rather depressing.

So, yes, you can say it doesn't matter who was right, Arius or Athanasius, if you like. But make no mistake about it: the implications of that shrug of the shoulders are far-reaching. If Arius was right, it means God is unknowable. It means human dignity and worth are nice ideas but have no foundation in reality. And it means the best God can do for us is to offer us a fine example and good advice.

There is, of course, a group which believes passionately that Arius was right, and that Athanasius only won by a power play. They are called Jehovah's Witnesses—very sincere and nice people, to be sure, but not following a faith known for its joyful exuberance. The reason for the difference is simple: Athanasius offers the world really good news, the Jehovah's Witnesses don't.

Finally, if this ancient debate really doesn't matter, then the motion of the last General Synod, that the blessing of same-sex unions does not go "against core doctrine (in the creedal sense)" is really a joke in rather poor taste, and nobody should take it terribly seriously. Doctrines do not come much more "core" and "creedal" than Athanasius's claim that Jesus was God incarnate.

29

Impossible Things before Breakfast 1

Born of the Virgin Mary

My wife and I have always loved etymologies. I have a little notebook from when we first met at university containing a list of interesting words to look up. And when we were married and had children, the Oxford Etymological Dictionary was always at hand for quick reference at mealtimes. One of the most interesting word origins I know is of the word "creed." Many people know it comes from the Latin credo, *"I believe." But it was an eye-opener when, many years ago, someone pointed out that* credo *has its own etymology. It is made up of the two Latin words* cor *(heart) and* dare *(to give). My creed, what I believe, is that to which I give my heart.*

This sermon, given in my own church of St. John the Evangelist, in April 2013, was part of a series on the creed.

At one point in Lewis Carroll's *Alice in Wonderland*, Alice says to the Red Queen: "One can't believe impossible things."

And the queen replies, "I daresay you haven't had much practice. . . . When I was your age, I always did it for half-an-hour a day. Why, sometimes I've believed as many as six impossible things before breakfast."[1]

The Red Queen, it's worth noticing, is totally insane.

---

1. Carroll, *Annotated Alice*, 215.

Sometimes saying the creed can feel like that—being asked to believe, not six impossible things, but twenty impossible things, and if not before breakfast, at least before lunch. And today's topic, what's usually called "the virgin birth," is a classic example.

Let's clear up a couple of things first. Although this subject is called the "virgin birth," it's really the virgin conception: that's where the miracle is supposed to have happened. Nobody claims there was anything miraculous about Jesus' birth! Secondly, it's not the same as "the immaculate conception." That is a Roman Catholic belief that Mary the mother of Jesus was conceived sinless—so that when the time came she would be (as it were) "a pure vessel" to receive the Son of God. But this isn't a belief shared by the rest of the church—for one thing, there's nothing in the Bible to suggest it—so we won't spend time on it this morning.

So here we are: "He was conceived by the Holy Spirit, born of the Virgin Mary"[2]—it does sound a bit far-fetched, doesn't it? Modern people have several problems with this idea:

- Virgins don't get pregnant. A woman gets pregnant, and you don't find yourself wondering, "Well, maybe this is another of those virgin conceptions. I suppose it's just possible there was a guy involved. You never know these days." And that leads to the second thing we think:

- Miracles don't happen. In those days, so runs the argument, they didn't understand about the laws of nature—so if something odd happened (an eclipse, or an earthquake, say), instead of wondering what the scientific explanation was, they would more likely say, "Well, this is God at work, trying to tell us something. It's a miracle, it's a sign, it's a warning." But of course these days we know what causes eclipses and earthquakes, so we don't need the idea of God to explain these things.

- Historians also tell us that, in those days, to say someone had a divine father and a human mother was a well-known way of emphasizing they were really important: it was said of many famous men (and it was generally men!) from the philosopher Plato to the emperor Caesar Augustus. So, goes the argument, that's why the Jesus story is told this way—simply to show how important he is—and we're being naïve if we take such things literally.

- And then there's the fact that only Matthew and Luke out of the whole New Testament talk about the conception of Jesus. Mark's Gospel says nothing about it and neither does John's Gospel; and there is no mention of it in anything St. Paul wrote. If it was true, don't you think

2. The Apostles' Creed.

everyone would have heard about it and it would be important enough that it would be mentioned lots of times in the New Testament?

Because of these things, many people think the story of the virgin conception of Jesus is just an ancient legend: it's not true. No modern, educated, sophisticated person (like us!) should have to say (or believe) such a ridiculous thing. So probably the best thing—if we need a creed at all—would be to make up our own, something we really can believe.

Is there another way to think about this? I happen to think there is. A famous philosopher once said, "life must be understood backwards."[3] So instead of beginning with Jesus' birth, let's start with the end of the story: Easter.

All through Jesus' ministry, there had been hints that he was more than a man, even a very good man. There are lots of examples. The Old Testament described God as a good shepherd who is concerned about his lost sheep: when Jesus was explaining his work, he told a story about a shepherd who went looking for a lost sheep. When he forgave sins, and people complained that only God could forgive sins, he ignored the comment. Jesus told parables about God's great banquet for all nations, but then, when people got a taste of that banquet with Jesus, who was the host? Jesus was. When he told a man who'd been healed to go home and tell people what God had done for him, the man went home and told what Jesus had done for him. He refers to the marriage of God with God's people, but then refers to himself as the bridegroom! And so on.[4]

Interesting! No wonder people often asked each other, "Who exactly is this?"

Of course, the crucifixion dashed their hopes: "we had hoped that he was the one to deliver Israel" (Luke 24:21)—but we can't believe that anymore. But then comes the resurrection, with lots of witnesses and many transformed lives, and those hints about who Jesus was suddenly begin to make sense. As a result, over time, Jesus comes to be seen, not just as the Messiah, but as the Creator of the universe taking on human form, the playwright writing a part for himself in the play, the cartoonist making herself a character in the cartoon strip. And quite soon, the question inevitably arises: If this is God come to our world, how did he get here? If Jesus is just a good man, then he got here like anyone else, of course, but if he really is (as we would say now) God incarnate, then the story Matthew and Luke tell of a divine origin and a human mother makes a lot more sense.

3. Kierkegaard, *Journals IV*, A.164.

4. There are many more such hints in John's Gospel, but the examples I have given are deliberately taken from the Synoptic Gospels.

So a lot hinges on this belief. Here's how the New Testament scholar N. T. Wright, explains his own conviction:

> If the first two chapters of Matthew and the first two of Luke had never existed, I do not suppose that my own Christian faith, or that of the church to which I belong, would have been very different.[There he is, saying his faith doesn't depend on the Christmas stories.] But since they do, and since for quite other reasons I have come to believe that the God of Israel, the world's creator, was personally and fully revealed in and as Jesus of Nazareth [he believes because of what he sees of the life, death and resurrection of Jesus!], I hold open my historical judgment and say: If that's what God deemed appropriate, who am I to object?[5]

And so many good things flow from this story. If it is true, it means our bodies are good—good enough for God to make one his home for nine months; it means bodily processes like pregnancy and birth are good things; it means being a woman, with a woman's body, is a good thing; and it means God is able to do amazing things through ordinary human beings who make themselves available! (I like the joke that says Mary was actually the fourth virgin the angel approached: but she was the first one to say yes.) When Mary said yes, the history of the whole world was changed!

You say, "Well, I'm still not convinced about this whole thing. Can I still consider myself a follower of Jesus if I'm not sure about this stuff?" Let me put it this way. The commonest word for a Christian in the New Testament is "disciple," which means learner or student or apprentice, which means being a Christian is actually belonging to a school. And if it's a school, there is learning to be done; there are Grade 1 lessons and there are graduate courses, and everything in between. And the person who is in Grade 1 of Jesus' school is just as much a Christian as the person doing graduate studies in Jesus' school! How come? Because the whole point of being in a school is that you don't know or understand—or believe—everything before you begin. That's why you're there, right? To learn? So can you be a follower of Jesus and be uncertain about some things? Of course.

So what do you do when it comes to the creed and you are expected to say these weird things?

---

5. N. T. Wright, "God's Way of Acting," para. 30. "According to the faith of the Church the Sonship of Jesus does not rest on the fact that Jesus had no human father: the doctrine of Jesus' divinity would not be affected if Jesus had been the product of a normal marriage. For the Sonship of which faith speaks is not a biological but an ontological fact, an event not in time but in God's eternity" (Ratzinger, *Introduction to Christianity*, 274–75).

a. Some people just don't say the things they don't believe. One pastor told me some people in his congregation say, "I believe in God" and then stop. Of course, if everybody did that, it could be rather embarrassing—one and a half minutes of silence. Or maybe after forty seconds, they'd suddenly say, "He was crucified under Pontius Pilate"—because they all believe that—and then silence again. There has to be a better way . . .

b. Two weeks ago, when we began thinking about the creed, I suggested it is a point form summary of the Christian story—just as, if every copy of *The Lion, the Witch and the Wardrobe* disappeared overnight, we could make up a list of twenty points that would remind us of the important parts of it. But if you began leaving bits out of it—"I don't like the idea of winter with no Christmas, so I won't tell that part of the story," or "I'm not really sure if Aslan came back to life, so I won't say that," what have you done? Basically, you have ruined the story: it doesn't make sense anymore. So with the creed: it's not a list of a dozen incredible things chosen at random to test how gullible we can be persuaded to be. It's a story we have received, a story we try to guide our lives by, and a story that we want to pass on to others. Why? Because it gives life! So I don't think silence is the answer. Maybe a better idea is this: if you're not sure about something, you could say it quietly and pray to understand it and grow into it over time.

c. The other thing that helps me is when we say the creed with the words "We believe" instead of "I believe." It reminds me it's not just me as a private individual trying to understand the Christian story. What God wants to do is create a new community, and the creed is a statement by us as a community of the story that holds us together.

So if I am struggling with something in the creed, I don't do so alone. Where I am weak in faith, others are strong; where others are weak in faith, I may be strong. And of course those strengths and weaknesses change over time. After recent natural and human disasters, you may have a hard time even saying, "I believe in God." That's OK: for other people, their belief in God may be very strong right now—so this week they may carry you through the creed; next week, someone else may be struggling with the phrase "the resurrection of the dead" because they're faced with the death of a loved one—but for you it's a given and it's your turn to carry them through the creed. So we say the words as a community—maybe confidently and firmly, maybe quietly and uncertainly—and that's OK.

And so: "I believe—we believe—in Jesus Christ his only son, our lord. He was conceived by the Holy Spirit and born of the Virgin Mary." Let's find ways to grow into it. It's part of our story, and the story is one that God means to give us life, and to give us joy.

30

Impossible Things before Breakfast 2

He Descended into Hell

IN THE FALL OF 2008, *The Morning Star ran a series of editorials by faculty on the items of the Creed. Why did I keep getting the awkward ones? My strategy with such things is normally to try to step back and see the subject in the context of the big story of the gospel. That almost always helps to put such difficult topics into perspective, even if it doesn't answer all the questions. That's what I tried to do here.*

Is life a comedy or a tragedy? Surely there is more to weep over than to laugh at in our world—but that is not the whole story.

Tragedy begins with a situation where the hero (Macbeth, for example) begins to rise in power and influence, like an arc beginning to ascend. But then, because of an internal flaw, he overreaches himself (Macbeth kills the king in order to become king himself), and the whole structure he has built comes tumbling down, often killing the hero as it does so. That's tragedy.

Comedy is the opposite. This time, early on in the story, things begin to go wrong. In a Shakespearian comedy, for example, people lose their way, identities are mistaken, and characters fall in love with the wrong person. The whole story seems to be moving in an endless downward slide. But by the end, of course, a corner has been turned: true identities are revealed, people are reunited with their true loves, and all's well that ends well.

Each kind of story describes a different trajectory: tragedy is an arc with its zenith at the top, comedy an arc with its nadir at the bottom. I explained this to my children when they were quite young, and my daughter said brightly, "Oh, you mean like a smiley face and a frowny face." I'd never thought of it that way, but of course, she was right. (She often is.)

So: Is life a comedy or a tragedy? That depends entirely on your worldview. And, as C. S. Lewis says, we can't figure out on our own which kind of play it is.[1] We can't tell from looking around whether we are in act 1 or act 5, who the principal actors are, and certainly not the outcome. We may find comic or tragic events in any given scene, but we are not in a position to see the play as a whole. For that, we need the playwright to show us the script. In other words, we need revelation.

God's supreme revelation in Jesus Christ shows us a God who "came down from heaven" (already the creed gives us an idea which direction the arc is going)—not like a spaceman traveling millions of miles through time and space, but (to paraphrase Lewis again) more like the author of the play writing a part for himself in the script.[2] The Creator stoops, he descends, he con-descends, to enter our human condition.

But things will get worse before they get better. The author-in-the-play becomes poor (2 Cor 8:9), he is "despised and rejected by others" (Isa 53:3), he is misunderstood by his students, and then betrayed into the hands of wicked men by one he had counted a friend.

Yet we are still not at the nadir: the arc must go lower yet. He is tried by a kangaroo court, sentenced to death by a callous Roman governor who cares nothing for justice. Then he is nailed naked to a vertical stake, to die in the Middle Eastern midday sun from asphyxiation, dehydration, and blood loss, by the most vicious form of execution ever devised by sinful human beings. As the creeds tersely put it, "he suffered death and was buried."

Surely that is the worst that can happen? If the arc is ever to start on an upward movement, you might think this would be the moment. Otherwise this is unmitigated tragedy. But no: there is one step lower that he has yet to go: "he descended into hell."

This phrase was not introduced into the Apostles' Creed till the fourth century, and it remains perhaps the most misunderstood clause in our creeds. It needs to be said first that the word "hell" does not mean the place of final punishment, which it has exclusively meant since the seventeenth

---

1. C. S. Lewis, "The World's Last Night," 61.
2. C. S. Lewis, *Surprised by Joy*, 181.

century. It is a translation of the Greek *hades* (close in meaning to the Hebrew *sheol*), not the Hebrew word *gehenna*. *Hades*, or *sheol*, is the place for the spirits of the dead, in between their death and the day of resurrection. Hence in most modern versions of the creeds, it says "he descended to the dead."

What does it mean for Jesus to "descend" there? Our main source for this article and its meaning is an obscure passage in Peter (I do not apologize for calling it obscure since Calvin does so too):

> He was put to death in the body but made alive in the spirit, in which also he went and made a proclamation to the spirits in prison, who in former times did not obey, when God waited patiently in the days of Noah. (1 Pet 3:18b–19)

Wayne Grudem, in the Tyndale Commentary, says there are five ways to understand this passage, but I have other fish to fry, so consult him if you want to know what they are. For the sake of brevity, here is Calvin's conclusion (though even he is tentative). He believes Peter is speaking "to the effect that the manifestation of Christ's grace was made to godly spirits, and that they were thus endued with the life-giving power of the Spirit." He points out that the word for prison can also be translated "watchtower," so that the spirits who are awaiting resurrection are not prisoners but rather watchers, "watching in hope of the salvation promised them, as though they saw it afar off." (If you want to know why, if Calvin is right, Peter says these spirits "did not obey," well, check the commentary.)[3]

Whatever the details of the doctrine, the point is this: Christ not only died and was buried, but went "lower" (spatial metaphors can seem a little foolish but they are the best we've got), to the place where spirits wait between death and the final resurrection, to announce to them that death and sin were finally conquered, and that the day of resurrection was at last on the way.

Now the upward swing begins: having swooped down from the highest to the lowest (more spatial metaphors), Jesus then begins the ascent of resurrection, ascension, and glorification, until the arc reaches its highest point—that point at the Father's right hand from which it began—and the story is complete.

Some call this way of describing the story "the swoop of grace." You can see why.

---

3. Calvin, *Hebrews and 1 and 2 Peter*, 293.

the swoop of grace

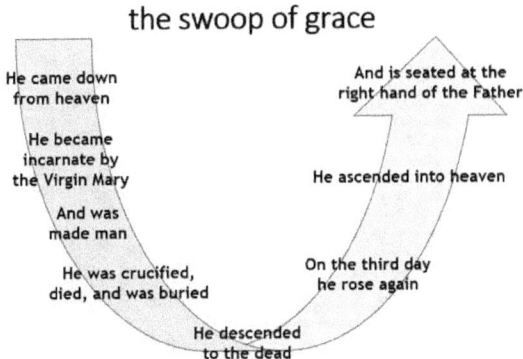

And what kind of story is this? A comedy, of course. A divine comedy—indeed, *the* divine comedy—describing an arc which begins higher and stoops lower than any other comedy ever could, a comedy that begins and ends in the heart of God.

My opening question, however, was, "Is life a comedy or a tragedy?," not, "Is the career of Jesus Christ a tragedy or a comedy?" But of course the two cannot be separated. Certainly the human story in this world began tragically, as humankind, in the tradition of every tragic hero, tried to rise beyond what we were made for, overreached our abilities, and were brought low through our fatal flaw.

But as grace dives down into our tragedy, we are caught up with Jesus and rescued from the inevitable end of every other tragedy. Through him, in that downward movement of incarnation, death, burial, and descent to the dead, and then the glorious upward swoop of his resurrection, ascension, and glorification, our story is turned into a comedy. And in the deepest sense of all, "all's well that ends well."

31

Impossible Things before Breakfast 3

On the Third Day He Rose Again

THIS SERMON WAS PREACHED *at St. John the Evangelist on the first Sunday after Easter in 2003. The Gospel reading was the story of Doubting Thomas.*

Let me tell you about the sermon I'm not going to preach today. It is based on the story of Thomas, and it goes like something this. "Maybe you consider yourself a doubter. Well, so was Thomas in today's reading. And clearly, Jesus accepted him, loved him, and solved his doubts. In the same way, Jesus accepts us too with all our doubts. Unfortunately, we don't exactly get to touch Jesus' hands in the way Thomas did. However, Jesus has not forgotten us. He says that, in our case, we must just believe anyway. And we can be encouraged because he does promise a blessing for folks like us who 'do not see and yet believe.'"

I don't know how you feel about that sermon, but the reason I dislike it is that, to be honest, it seems a bit of a rip-off. Personally, I'd be willing to give up 10 percent of the blessing for 10 percent more certainty. In fact, some people think that approach of saying, "Switch off your mind and just believe blindly" is so un-Christian as to be heresy! It even has its own name: fideism. So don't worry if you feel that "just believing" is impossible for you. You are actually avoiding heresy, even though you probably didn't realize it. Good work.

Are there actually reasons for believing in the resurrection? It seems so way out of left field to most normal people. I remember once doing a debate with a philosophy professor in Montreal. In the course of the debate, I said something about Jesus coming back from death, and he immediately shot back, "Sure, Jesus is alive. You mean like Elvis?" So is that what the resurrection means? A combination of wishful thinking, sentimentality, and superstition, on a level with thinking that Elvis is alive?

Let me offer you six ways I have come across for thinking about the resurrection which might be more helpful than simply being told to "believe anyway."

1. THE HISTORICAL APPROACH

Some people begin to believe by considering the historical evidence for the resurrection. My wife became a Christian while a student at Oxford, under the influence of some friends who had themselves recently come to faith in Jesus, and they gave her books on this subject. Her conclusion, like that of many others who have followed that route, was Jesus must indeed have risen from the dead, and that therefore she should follow him.

Here's just one of many historical factors to consider. New Testament scholar N. T. Wright has written an 800-page book on the resurrection, *Jesus and the Victory of God*. He points out that, at the time of Jesus, there were dozens of so-called "Messiahs" around, and not a few of them ended up getting crucified. However, in all cases but one, once that happened, that was the end of the messianic movement. But in the case of Jesus, the opposite happened: the movement he started, instead of dying, grew until it reached the whole world. Something must have happened, but what was it? That's the question. The resurrection, impossible though it may seem, makes perfect sense of the data.

Now, of course, this is not the only way to approach the resurrection. If it were, the church would be full of historians. But I don't need to tell you there are historians who don't believe, and nonhistorians who do believe, though for other reasons. But this still seems to be a helpful avenue for some.

2. THE BUTTERFLY APPROACH

Then there are some people who say, "Hey, I don't have a problem with the resurrection. It happens all the time. Look at the spring: trees and flowers which seemed to be dead a few days before come to life, butterflies burst out of apparently lifeless chrysalises. There's resurrection for you. No problem."

Now, I confess I think this approach has some serious problems. It seems to me there is a world of difference between a seed that appears to be dead and a person who is actually dead. And seeds "come to life" millions of times every day, yet there is only one recorded instance of a human resurrection. So I don't think it's entirely a fair comparison.

At the same time, you might point out it is the same Creator who is behind the spring and the resurrection; and Jesus did say his death would be like a seed falling into the ground to die and then bearing fruit. So there is a kind of—what can we call it?—artistic style in the spring and the resurrection which is similar. So maybe this is an approach which will work for you.

3. THE CONSISTENCY APPROACH

Some people are helped by not centering out the question of the resurrection and looking at it as an isolated event. After all, whether you believe in the resurrection depends on what you believe about God. If there is no God, of course, it's highly unlikely there could be a resurrection. But, on the other hand, if there is a God like the God Jesus spoke about, then resurrection makes perfect sense. In fact, what would have been strange would have been if there had been no resurrection.

For this approach to work, the obvious questions are: Is there a God? And, if so, what is this God like? And what does this God think about Jesus? We have to consider these questions before we can approach the question of the resurrection as anything more than a weird and irrational idea.

4. THE EXPERIENCE APPROACH

Other people are helped by listening to people's stories when they say the living Jesus has had an effect on their lives. Three examples spring to mind:

- One friend of mine is a librarian and historian, and not the sort of person we generally think of as—what shall we say?—given to mindless religious fanaticism. Yet he says in a firm, matter-of-fact kind of way that Jesus changed his life.

- Another friend who grew up Jewish had a vision of the risen Jesus, and became a Christian. He is now an army chaplain, and served a term in Afghanistan. Again, not someone you would exactly identify with religious hysteria.

- A third friend is a criminal lawyer (not a group known for their gullibility) whose son was miraculously healed a few years ago in answer to prayer. The local newspaper wanted to write an article about it, with the headline. "God healed my son," but my friend said, "No, I want the headline to say, 'Jesus healed my son.'"

And there are so many stories like this. The question is: Do these stories ring true? I remember a sermon (one I did like) on Newton's second law of motion, which, if I remember rightly, says that a body moving in a particular direction will only change direction if impacted by a force from outside, moving in a different direction. That's what these people are saying: my life was going in one direction, then it changed direction, and I believe the outside force was Jesus. So what do we make of all this? For some, that's a fruitful approach to thinking about the resurrection.

5. THE IMAGINATIVE APPROACH

If the historical question appeals to the mind, this one appeals to the imagination. Some people find it helpful to do a thought experiment: not so much looking into the tomb to see if we can figure out what's there (or not) but rather standing at the door of the tomb and looking out at the world. How does the world look different if Jesus did rise? How would my life look different today? This week? How would death look different if Jesus did rise? Would it make more sense or less? Try it and see what happens.

Bishop John Spong once asked how any thoughtful person could expect his physicist daughter to believe in the resurrection, to which Bishop William Willimon replied, "How little imagination does his daughter now have?"[1]

Imagination is not against reason: but it can illuminate reason.

6. THE CHOICE APPROACH

My last suggestion is this. A friend in Ottawa is a senior civil servant. For years he went to church with his wife because she believed, and he wanted to be supportive. But he didn't have what he considered the necessary feelings to call himself a Christian. Then a mutual friend said, "Dave, faith isn't a matter of feelings. It's a matter of choice. You choose to believe." Dave isn't particularly into getting in touch with his feelings anyway, but the idea of

---

1. Cited in Mouw, *He Shines in All That's Fair*, 5.

choice is something that made sense to him. So he chose to believe, and his life changed. Maybe that is the approach that will work for you.

Having said all that, most people who do believe in the resurrection don't do so because of any single thing. Maybe that's true for all the most important things we believe in. After all, if I ask you why you think Canada is a great country, you won't give me a single answer. You might list your favorite things: the Rockies, the CBC, Shania Twain, the Maple Leafs (maybe). And all of our answers would be true because Canada is such a big part of us. So with the resurrection: it may be any combination of these six approaches (or any others, of course) that helps you.

It may be that you say, "Well, I still can't believe." Personally, I am encouraged that the first disciples also had a hard time believing, and yet they were still considered true disciples. After all, when Jesus first told them he would die and rise again, they basically told him, "Jesus, that's really not a smart idea." They just didn't get it. And even after forty days of appearances after the resurrection, as he was about to return to heaven, Luke tells us "and some doubted." These were the diehard doubters, far moreso than Thomas. And yet they are still called disciples.

Maybe our problem is we think of believing as a thing that happens in our minds. But John's Gospel uses the word "believe" more or less as the equivalent of "follow." So in Matthew, Mark, and Luke, Jesus says, "Follow me,"[2] whereas in John he says, "Believe in me." In other words, for John "believing," like "following," is something you do with your feet and your hands and your heart in the first place: the head figures things out afterwards.

And I'm encouraged by the fact that Jesus, like the good teacher he is, is patient with doubters—not just with Thomas but with those who doubted at his ascension—and with us too. My hunch is that we will always have doubts. In fact, doubts are good for us, because they help separate the wheat from the chaff in what we believe. We don't get extra brownie points from God for believing without question.

The thing to do with our doubts and questions is to do what those first disciples did: bring them to Jesus, and say, "Lord, I don't know whether I believe, I don't know what I believe, but I do want to learn to follow you, and I'm open to learning if you're open to teaching." And you know what? He is. And as John's Gospel promises, as we learn and follow, we will figure out what to believe and find "life in his name" (John 20:31).

---

2. Mark 1:17; cf. John 1:12 etc.

32

What on Earth is Justification?

LIKE MOST EVANGELICAL INSTITUTIONS, *Wycliffe College* has its own Statement of Faith. This one is called *The Six Principles*. But, as with most such statements, there is always discussion and even argument about what the various items mean. For this reason, one Fall, the faculty took it in turns to comment on each item in the Statement. I was assigned "Justification by the free grace of God through faith in Jesus Christ."

The approach I took comes from my passion for translation. This may in part be the influence of C. S. Lewis, who said once, "My task was . . . simply that of a translator."[1] That in turn got woven into my time as a campus evangelist, where I was constantly struggling with ways to make the gospel clear to students with no Christian background, and thus no understanding of Christian terminology such as "justification" or even "faith."

So you want to know about salvation by grace alone? It's all perfectly straightforward, really. The Thirty-Nine Articles spell out the meaning of this quintessential Reformation doctrine in classic terms. Here it is in black-and-white, "Article XI: Of the Justification of Man":

---

1. Lewis, "Rejoinder to Dr. Pittenger," 183.

> We are accounted righteous before God, only for the merit of our Lord and Savior Jesus Christ by Faith, and not for our own works or deservings: Wherefore, that we are justified by Faith only is a most wholesome Doctrine, and very full of comfort, as more largely is expressed in the Homily of Justification.[2]

If you are still confused, you could always check the appropriate homily. It is to be found in the book, *Sermons and Homilies Appointed to be Read in Churches*. These sermons date back to the sixteenth century, and were a way for the newly-minted Church of England to teach Reformed doctrine through clergy who were often uneducated and unskilled, and did not understand doctrine themselves. They could simply read these sermons. Two copies of the book, dated 1833, are to be found in the library. Here are the words of the Reformers on the topic of justification:

> In [Romans], the apostle toucheth specially three things, which must go together in our justification. Upon God's part, his great mercy and grace: upon Christ's part, justice; that is, the satisfaction of God's justice, or the price of our redemption, by the offering of his body, and shedding of his blood, with fulfilling of the law perfectly and thoroughly: and upon our part true and lively faith in the merits of Jesus Christ.[3]

The problem is that the words which made clear the meaning of the doctrine for the sixteenth century are not necessarily those that will cut it with the unchurched person today. (I count at least eighteen words in that definition which have changed their meaning since then.) Is there another way to say it? How about this: "There was once a man who had two sons. The younger one said to his father, 'Father, give me the share of the property that will belong to me'" (Luke 15:12). Yes, the parable of the prodigal son, a story that is timeless, that takes very little translation for people to "get it" in any culture.

Why this story? Because all of the homily's "three things" are there. There is God's grace and mercy: the son is welcomed back with unconditional open arms. There is no period of probation ("If you're still going straight in six months . . ."), there are no conditions ("Well, you can come home as long as . . ."), and no lectures ("If you knew what you have put me through . . ."). Just love, just relief, just thankfulness.

What about "the price of our redemption?" After all, there is no crucifixion in the story. But wait: What is "the price of our redemption" except

---

2. *The Book of Common Prayer*.
3. Corrie, *Certain Sermons, Appointed by the Queen's Majesty*, 21.

God's willingness to absorb the pain of our rebellion rather than punish us for our folly? Is this not the pain of "God . . . in Christ" on the cross? Where then is the cross in the story of the prodigal son? The cross is surely in the heart of the Father, who chooses to keep inside the intense pain this child has caused him, rather than unloading it in the form of wrath on the one who really deserved it.

And "true and lively faith?" In the story, this is no complicated theological concept. "True and lively faith" is this kid trudging along the hot, dusty road towards the only place he has even a chance of a square meal. It's hardly a definition of faith, but it is a great image of faith.

Of course, the writer of the homily attributes this understanding of salvation to "the apostle." But maybe those are correct who say that everything in Paul comes ultimately from Jesus, and that the Epistle to the Romans is just an extended commentary on the parable of the prodigal son.

33

What's Wrong with Amazing Grace?

SOMETIMES A SERMON IS *a good excuse for preachers to get something off their chest. That can be awkward if you are preaching in your regular congregation, because they will know what you are up to. ("Oh, here he goes again. It's going to be one of those.") It's easier when you are a guest preacher, doing a preach-and-run. Apart from anything else, this congregation is not surprised to get a one-off sermon, so they are less likely to realize you are actually using them as a pretext for exorcizing a grudge.*

In the present case, it was January 2007, and I was once again a guest at Knox Presbyterian Church in Toronto. Little did they realize I had been saving up my complaint against "Amazing Grace" to unburden on some unsuspecting congregation on just such an occasion. How did they feel about it? I don't know. But I certainly felt better. Isn't that what preaching is about?

What's wrong with amazing grace? The first and most important answer is: nothing. You need to know I believe in grace, and it is indeed amazing. Whether you consider yourself a follower of Jesus or not, you are here because of grace, you are alive because of grace. If you wake up tomorrow morning and get to live another day, that will be because of grace. What is grace? Grace is God's amazing generosity to a world that does not deserve

God's generosity, cannot buy God's generosity, and (generally) does not expect God's generosity.

Of course, if you are a follower of Jesus Christ, you know more than that about grace: you know that God forgave your sins when that was the last thing you deserved, that God has welcomed you into his family, made you his friend, taken you into his confidence about his plans for the world, and encourages you to be his apprentice in turning the world right side up. That's amazing, and that's grace!

But I do have some problems with the song called "Amazing Grace," because I actually think grace is bigger and therefore more amazing than the song lets on.

Let's start with the song. It is beloved of so many, in and out of the church. How can anyone find anything wrong with it? The first thing that might cause us to wonder is the fact the song is so popular in secular circles! Here are about twenty randomly selected names of artists who have recorded this song: Andy Griffith, Ani Difranco, Billy Ray Cyrus, Christina Aguilera, Daniel Lanois, Diana Ross, Dolly Parton, Janis Joplin, Jerry Garcia, Joan Baez, Judy Collins, Kylie Minogue, Pete Seeger, Rod Stewart, Woody Guthrie, and Willie Nelson.

I don't want to be mean or judgmental, but I am not aware of any of them claiming to be followers of the Jesus who brought amazing grace to the world. That's not necessarily bad: after all, maybe God will use the song to nudge them (and their fans) toward Jesus. But would they sing it if it were a bit more challenging?

So what could possibly be wrong with it?

- It's interesting there is no reference to Jesus or his cross. The way Christians understand God's grace, it is in Jesus that we see the grace of God most clearly: that God would go to such lengths for us. When we think "grace," we don't just think a benevolent, grandfatherly, "as long as they're happy" kind of kindness. We think of a man 2,000 years ago who suffered a brutal execution. Maybe one reason secular singers like it is that it doesn't mention the dreaded J-word or that messy execution.

- The song is more about me than about God (the words "I," "me" and "mine" come three times in each of the first four verses). But Christian spirituality is not all about me. I am not denying that's a part of it, naturally: that God should graciously pay attention to little ol' sinful me. But I am not where grace begins and I am not where grace ends.

  Grace begins in the heart of God before the world was ever made, and it involves the whole world, and will end with the renewal of the whole world. By grace, God sweeps me up to be a part of that—that's the thrill of amazing grace—but it's not all about me! Because of our sinful nature and the emphasis in our culture on "me" (think of all those uses of "my" in Windows, for example: "My documents," "My music," "My pictures," "My video" etc.—my computer comes with ten such folders), it is easy to become obsessed with this piece of the puzzle, and forget we're not at the heart of it.

- Lastly, there is no reference to what we do in this world if we have experienced grace. Grace here has nothing to do with living a lifestyle of grace in this world: it's just a vehicle to get us through this world unscathed as quickly as possible, to survive the "dangers, toils and snares." I can't wait to get to heaven and escape from this vale of tears. Get me out of here as quickly as possible! I don't think that's exactly the attitude that Jesus encouraged in his disciples.

Now, we need to say that this song makes better sense if we know the story of the writer, John Newton. For him, Jesus was very clearly the center of his faith. If this song seems a lot about "me," it's because of his experience. He was a slave trader, carrying slaves from Africa to North America, who turned to God when his ship was about to sink during a terrible storm on the Atlantic. He really felt he was a terrible wretch. He was amazed to discover God didn't treat him as he deserved, he was amazed he was still alive, and he was amazed God could love someone like him.

Neither was he a man who was so heavenly minded as to be no earthly use. His belief in heaven actually led him to work for the abolition of the slave trade he had once supported, and when William Wilberforce was wondering whether he should become an ordained minister or fight against slavery in the British Parliament, Newton encouraged him to stay in parliament and serve God there—which changed the course of world history. So there is no question about it: Newton personally did not embody my three complaints. Far from it.

Having said that, at the same time, I want to say grace is more than the song says, and more amazing than that!

1. WHAT ABOUT COMMON GRACE?

Where to begin? The words of Jesus would seem like a sensible place to start. In the Sermon on the Mount, for example, one thing Jesus is teaching about is the importance of loving our enemies. The way he explains it is interesting: he tells us what God is like, and then says we should be the same. Love your enemies. Why? Because God loves his enemies. How do we know God loves his enemies? Because he sends Jesus to die for our sins? Well, that is true, of course, but it is not what Jesus says. He actually says:

> Love your enemies and pray for those who persecute you, so that you may be children of your Father in heaven [he wants to remake us in the image of God]: for [because] he makes his sun rise on the evil and on the good, and sends rain on the righteous and on the unrighteous. (Matt 5:44–45)

God blesses the righteous and the unrighteous equally. Of course, it may not be as simple as that. There is an old rhyme which says:

> The rain it raineth every day
> upon the just and unjust fella;
> but rather more upon the just
> for the unjust hath the just's umbrella.

But the point Jesus is making is that God is indiscriminate in his goodness, blesses people in a thousand ways, whoever they are, whatever they've done, and whatever they think of God! That's amazing, and (guess what) that's grace.

The apostle Paul taught the same as his Master. In Acts 14:17, he says: "God has not left himself without a witness in doing good—giving you rains from heaven and fruitful seasons, and filling you with food and your hearts with joy." He is preaching to unbelievers, and he explains to them that God has blessed them with material blessings. Why? For the simple reason that they can be satisfied and joyful. Amazing, eh? This is God's grace, as much as the grace that flows from the cross of Jesus Christ. In fact, they are sides of the same coin, or two points along the same continuum. Both are expressions of God's love, both are grace, and both are amazing. Maybe somebody could write a song about that.

Why does this matter? One reason is if we don't understand this, we won't understand what is happening in our world, and that will shake our faith. I did some research a few years back on why young people leave church once they leave home.[1] One of the themes that emerged was that a number of them said things like this (and I paraphrase):

> Once I got out into the world, to my surprise I found a lot of people who were actually good people: they were intelligent, caring, forgiving, thoughtful, and funny. They had good marriages and solid friendships (at least, as many as Christians do), did their jobs creatively and conscientiously, and gave to charity.

---

1. This was published as *Growing Up Christian*.

All my life, I'd been taught that because they are sinners, and the world is a bad place, they would all be mean, spiteful, greedy, and lustful all the time, and it simply wasn't the case.

As a result, their faith faltered, and in some cases disappeared. But if they had had a doctrine of this kind of grace—common grace, as Reformed folk call it—their faith would not have been shaken. They would simply have said, "Wow, this is wonderful: God is blessing these people so much! Yes, they are sinners like everyone else; yes, they need to trust in Christ for their salvation. But God loves them anyway: all these good things in their lives are gifts of God's grace, but they don't realize it yet."

In Paul's mind, common grace and saving grace are connected: in Romans 2, he asks: "Do you not realize that God's kindness is meant to lead you to repentance?" Some people are brought to Christ because they have a sense of guilt and are looking for forgiveness, others because they have a sense of emptiness in their lives and realize only God can fill it: but it sounds as though Paul is saying some have experienced amazing blessings from God, and a proper sense of gratitude ought to bring them in faith to God. If God's grace to me in creation is amazing, how much more his grace in salvation!

2. WHAT ABOUT PREVENIENT GRACE?

There's another dimension to this grace business, and it links common grace (God's material care for everyone) and saving grace (God's love through the death of Christ). This aspect is what John Wesley called prevenient grace. What he meant by this was that God is at work preparing people's hearts to hear about Christ, nudging them, drawing them, trying to catch their attention, causing them to think about questions of faith. This happens long before the person deliberately says, "Yes, I want to trust Christ." It's the kind of grace that clears the stones out of the field, ploughs up the ground, sows the seed, waters the seed, and waits patiently for a harvest. We might add, it is this kind of prevenient grace which makes people question the meaning of life; it's prevenient grace that makes them wonder why they can't forgive more easily; it's prevenient grace which makes people look at the stars and say, "There must be a God out there."

This is the kind of grace Paul banks on in Acts 17. He doesn't start in by talking about sin and the Athenians' need for a Savior. He talks first of all about three ways God has been trying to get their attention.

- There is the altar to the unknown god (23): God has convinced them there is a god whom they do not know. Paul can tell them this God's name.

- Then he quotes things from their own religion—truths they have figured out (with the help of prevenient grace): in verse 25 he speaks of God as the source of everything (which the Stoics believed) and God not needing our help (which the Epicureans believed). You can imagine them nodding as he said these things.

- Then thirdly, in verse 28, he quotes from their poets Aratus and Epimenides: "In him we live and move and have our being" and "We too are his offspring." Now these poets were actually writing in praise of the pagan god Zeus, not the God of Jesus: but Paul has no hesitation about saying (in effect), "Actually they were writing not about Zeus but about the Creator God of the Jews. They just didn't know it."

How was Paul able to do this? First of all, he knew that, somewhere in this pagan culture, God was at work, because he believed in prevenient grace. Then he says, "As I walked about your city and looked carefully at the objects of your worship, I found . . ." (Acts 17:23). So he looked carefully to see what clues God had planted, or, if you prefer, to see where prevenient grace was at work, so he could show the Athenians how it pointed to saving grace as found in Christ. If we don't look for these things, we won't find them.

I suppose I came to these convictions about grace through doing the work of evangelism in the universities. I discovered that if I lectured on the resurrection, nobody came. But if I lectured on "Jesus is Alive, Elvis is Alive: What's the Difference?" people were fascinated.

A useful example that came along was the cartoon strip, *Overboard*. I don't know if you have ever seen it, but it's about three pirates and their Labrador dog Louie, on their pirate ship. Occasionally, an extra character turns up: he sits at a drawing board, and there is a sign on the wall saying "Overboard Inc." Who is he? Well, he's the creator, and the characters come and argue about him: sometimes they don't like the lines he gives them, sometimes they want to write the story themselves, sometimes he lets them experience the results of their foolish choices. Now, if I tried to talk about the incarnation to secular students, people would just think it sounded weird. If, on the other hand, I talked about the divine Artist writing himself into the cartoon strip people call Life, they understood. Even a cartoon strip can be a gift of prevenient grace, just waiting for us to notice it.

So, three aspects of grace. I won't call them three kinds of grace, because they all show the love of a generous God.

- First, there is saving grace, when we put our trust in Christ and are caught up into God's purposes for the world. That is where John Newton's experience began.

But then there are:

- Common grace: God's material blessings on all humankind regardless of whether they believe or not; and
- Prevenient grace, God at work in the world, preparing the ground for people to understand and trust Jesus.

We need to understand all three of them: if we only stress common grace and prevenient grace, we will neglect the cross. But if we stress the cross and forget the other aspects of God's grace, we will be puzzled by the way ungodly people are blessed, and (maybe worse) we won't see how God is at work in people's lives or be able to point them to Christ.

Let's rejoice in God's grace, wherever we find it, and cooperate with this God whose grace is so amazing.

G

Good News about Evangelism

When I was hired at Wycliffe College, I asked if I could please be called something other than Professor of Evangelism. "No," I was told: "your job is to redeem the word." Sigh.

Well, the word "evangelism" has been around for some 300 years, but it continues to divide people inside and outside churches, not only about how it should be done but (in some quarters at least) whether it should be done at all. I can't help reflecting rather wryly that the word "evangelism" is never used in the New Testament. The references there are to the message of the gospel (the evangel), the activity of sharing good news (evangelizing), and the person who shares it (the evangelist). Even that knowledge might begin to shift our perspective.

A lot of my work—somewhat to my surprise—in the past twenty years has been to do what I was told on that occasion, to try and redeem the idea of evangelism. Yes, there is bad evangelism, just as there are bad marriages, bad politics, and bad education. But we don't give up on those things just because of that. Here are some of themes I have worked on for those twenty years.

34

Humanizing Evangelism

John 1: 35–51

I LOVE CHURCH PLANTING. Not that I have ever done it, though if I had my time over again, I would love to help with starting a new church. I have even taught courses on church planting, because I think it is so important. I do know enough, however, to do it in partnership with a real, flesh-and-blood, church-planting practitioner. I am great at the theory, but unsurprisingly that's not enough.

I also enjoy hanging out with church planters and church plants. So a few years back, in the spring of 2016, it was a great joy to be invited to preach at a relatively new church plant in my own city of Hamilton. Although the church is (more or less) Baptist, it is called Eucharist. (Go figure.) The topic was evangelism.

For about the past fifty years, evangelism has had a bad rap. Becky Manley Pippert wrote over forty years ago: "There was a part of me that secretly felt evangelism was something you shouldn't do to your dog, let alone a friend."[1] Many Christians felt the same—and many still do.

---

1. Pippert, *Out of the Saltshaker*, 16.

But if we understand it properly, evangelism is not an option—it's an important part of being a follower of Jesus. You could even say it's a spiritual discipline. How come?

At the heart of Christianity is a spoken message—the gospel, or good news. So what is that good news? That you can have a personal relationship with God? Yes, that's part. That your sins can be forgiven? Thanks to be to God, yes. That there is life beyond death? Yes, but it's more than that. The good news is that through Jesus Christ, his death, and his resurrection, God is putting right everything that is wrong in the world, and you and I are invited to be part of that process. That includes forgiveness, a personal relationship with God, and life after death, but also includes giving our lives to playing our part in that work.

So why is evangelism important? Because evangelism is telling people this is what's going on, telling people what God is like, what God is up to, and inviting them to say yes to Jesus' invitation. So if that talking doesn't happen, without someone saying something, nobody knows this is what's going on, and the whole thing doesn't work. In fact, you and I are here this morning because, somewhere along the way, someone talked to us, and we thought it was worth checking out.

Having said that, there are different ways to do evangelism. As C. S. Lewis says, "There are many different ways of bringing people into [God's] kingdom, even some ways that I specially dislike."[2]

This story (John 1:35–51) is about a form of evangelism—I'm not sure what to call it, but maybe "relational" or just "human" is the best word. So, four examples of evangelism happening to human beings in relationships.

a. The First Invitation: Andrew and John (vv. 35–39)

> The next day John again was standing with two of his disciples, and as he watched Jesus walk by, he exclaimed, 'Look, here is the Lamb of God!' The two disciples heard him say this, and they followed Jesus. When Jesus turned and saw them following, he said to them, 'What are you looking for?' They said to him, 'Rabbi' (which translated means Teacher), 'where are you staying?' He said to them, 'Come and see.' They came and saw where he was staying, and they remained with him that day. It was about four o'clock in the afternoon.

---

2. Lewis, "Cross Examination," 262.

The whole sequence of events in this chapter is triggered by John the Baptist. He points Jesus out to them, and they immediately leave John and follow after Jesus. (That's worth a whole separate sermon, but it'll have to be another time.)

I was discussing this story with a minister friend, and he said, "Of course they weren't saved at this point." Frankly, I'm not so sure. After all, John says they "follow." I think he is using that word as a signal that they are already disciples, because a disciple is basically someone who follows. Sure, they are disciples who don't know very much and haven't had any experience of discipleship, but they're doing the most basic thing disciples do: follow. That's what's important.

Jesus realizes they're there and turns around, and asks, "What are you looking for?" It's a reasonable enough question, isn't it? "Can I help you?" They don't know what to say. I suppose they could have said something sensible like, "Well, our teacher said you were the Lamb of God, but we have no idea what that means." Instead, the way I see it, they are stuck for words, and just stammer out, "Errrr . . . rabbi, where are you staying?"—which is perhaps the first thing that comes to their mind.

Now—you may know this already—one of the things that's unique about John's Gospel compared with the other three is John likes to play with words, particularly second meanings. So, he uses "stay" or "remain" twice more in these verses: "They came and saw where he was staying, and they remained with him that day."

If you know the older translations of the Bible, like the King James, you'll know what I'm getting at if I translate it this way: "Rabbi, where are you abiding? . . . They saw where he was abiding and they abode with him that day." Do you see what's going on?

This same word occurs later in John (chapter 15), where Jesus tells the disciples the secret to surviving and thriving as a Christian. He says, "abide in me." It's the same word. The Message says, "make your home in me." So back in chapter 1, when Jesus says to Andrew and John, "Come and see," he's effectively saying, "Come and see where I'm making my home." And John tells us, "They made their home with him for that day." So right at the beginning of their knowing Jesus, they learn the key to becoming and staying a disciple: making their home wherever Jesus has his home.

Let's go back to their question: "Where are you staying?" He could have said, "That's a rather personal question," or, "I'll be teaching in the synagogue on Sabbath: come then and I'll explain." No. He says a much more vulnerable thing: "Come and see." (Philip will use the same words in verse 46.)

Jesus invites them home for—well, for what? I have asked audiences in North America and in Kenya, and they will usually say, "He evangelized them," or "He preached to them." Well, frankly, he didn't need to take them home to do that.

But there's a clue here: it's four o'clock. What do civilized people do at four in the afternoon? They have tea, obviously! Alright, so I'm pretty sure it wasn't tea. But I would be surprised if they didn't share a drink and a meal. And I have no doubt they talked. Did they ask him questions? I'm sure they did. "What on earth did John mean when he said you were the lamb of God?" Did he ask them questions? Well, duh. Did Jesus ever not ask questions?

As a result, something happens to them. You see the change in Andrew straight away:

b. The Second Invitation: Andrew and Peter (vv. 41–42)

> Andrew first found his brother Simon and said to him, "We have found the Messiah" . . . He brought Simon to Jesus, who looked at him and said, "You are Simon son of John. You are to be called Cephas" (which is translated Peter).

"We have found the Messiah!" Five words of good news! It's really a very minimal statement of faith, isn't it? But (and here's another thing about John), John has low standards when it comes to who is and is not a real Christian.

Just one other example: The woman at the well in chapter 4 only asks a question: "Can he be the Messiah?"—less definite than Andrew, even! Does that make her a believer? Well, she tells what Jesus has done for her—she gives her testimony, and others believe through her—and for John, testimony is one sign of being a true believer. So here Andrew testifies too, and his testimony is very simple. Over the years, his understanding will fill out—if you ask him five years down the road what he means by saying "Jesus is the Messiah," his answer will be very different from what it is today—but this is a great starting point, and that's all Jesus needs. The divine camel has his nose in the tent of Andrew's life.

So Andrew brings Peter. It's interesting we're not told anything about what Peter thinks or says or does. Unlike Andrew, Peter doesn't call Jesus the Messiah. In fact, for once Peter says nothing—which is unusual for him. But we are told what Jesus does and says: Jesus looked at him. Wouldn't we love to know what that look was! Obviously there was something about it that made John think it was worth writing it down.[3]

I would guess Jesus is sizing him up, and seeing something of who Peter really is—or who he can become through his discipleship. Then Jesus renames him—not Simon, but Cephas/Peter, the Rock. Still today, people sometimes take a new name when they're baptized—a sign of being a new person with a new life.

c. Jesus and Philip (v. 45a)

> The next day Jesus decided to go to Galilee. He found Philip and said to him, "Follow me."

John says Jesus went to Galilee and found Philip. What does that suggest? Jesus was looking for him. So what's that about? Well, we are told Philip is from Bethsaida, just like Andrew and Peter. My guess is they knew each other, and perhaps they suggested him to Jesus. ("Jesus, we have a friend we think would like to meet you.") So they go to Galilee, they look for Philip, they find him, he's invited to "follow," and he does.

As with Peter, there's nothing here about what Philip said or did on this occasion. But we do know what he did next: it's in verse 45. I can't help looking down the road of Philip's life, and seeing that, by the time we get to the book of Acts, he is actually called Philip the evangelist (Acts 21:8).[4] Here is his first attempt at evangelism. It's kind of awkward—but it works.

d. Philip and Nathanael (vv. 45b–49)

> Philip found Nathanael and said to him, "We have found him about whom Moses in the law and also the prophets wrote, Jesus son of Joseph from Nazareth."

Just as Jesus found Philip, so Philip "found" Nathanael, and presumably for the same reason: he knew him already, and he was pretty sure Nathanael would be interested.

For the one and only time, the person being evangelized doesn't respond immediately. (Thank goodness! I don't know about you, but that is far more often the reaction I get to my attempts to evangelize!) Nathanael

---

3. Luke also notes a time when Jesus looked hard at Peter, but the circumstances are very different (22:61).

4. Only one of three uses of the word in the New Testament.

is skeptical, actually sarcastic: "Can anything good come out of Nazareth?" The implication seems to be, "Philip, are you crazy? This can't possibly be right."

I'm encouraged to see Philip (even though he will become "the evangelist") doesn't know what to say. It's a common fear in evangelism ("I wouldn't know what to say") and often my own experience. In fact, he's done the best he could, he's said the thing that's most important to him from his encounter with Jesus. He is the one "about whom Moses in the law and also the prophets wrote." After that, he's run out of apologetic arguments. But that's OK. He says the only reasonable thing left for him to say: "Come and see for yourself." Which Nathanael does.

> When Jesus saw Nathanael coming towards him, he said of him, 'Here is truly an Israelite in whom there is no deceit!' Nathanael asked him, 'Where did you come to know me?' Jesus answered, 'I saw you under the fig tree before Philip called you.' Nathanael replied, 'Rabbi, you are the Son of God! You are the King of Israel!'

It's interesting that Jesus doesn't answer Nathanael's argument. He doesn't give three compelling reasons why it's OK for the Messiah to come from Nazareth. No, Jesus has supernatural insight into Nathanael's character and Nathanael is bowled over! Miracles are really good acid for dissolving people's skepticism—far better than argument. And Nathanael goes straight from being the most dubious of the lot to making the strongest statements about Jesus of all of them. Let's put them side by side:

> Andrew: "We have found the Messiah." (41)
> Philip: "We have found him about whom Moses in the law and also the prophets wrote, Jesus son of Joseph from Nazareth." (45)
> Nathanael: "Rabbi, you are the Son of God! You are the King of Israel!" (49)

And what does Jesus say?

> "This impresses you? You will see greater things than these." (50)

Basically, "You ain't seen nothing yet! This is just the beginning." And of course, it is.

So, four cases of someone being evangelized in relationship. I notice first that:

   a. There are some things all these stories have in common:

- In each case there is a personal encounter. That encounter is not brought about by great preaching, or going to a lively worship service, or reading apologetics literature. Not that there is anything wrong with those, of course, but here we see the power of the personal encounter.

- The second thing I observe may sound odd, but it's this: in each case, words are spoken. I say this because I often have people quote to me some words attributed to St. Francis: "Preach the gospel at all times. If necessary, use words." But no, apart from anything else, it is highly unlikely Francis ever said such a thing.[5] No, words are necessary, as they were for Jesus. As Ed Stetzer puts it, "using that statement is a bit like saying, 'Feed the hungry at all times. If necessary, use food.'"[6]

- The third thing is that all these men become lifelong disciples—apprentices of Jesus, being trained in the ways of the kingdom. "Christian" and "disciple" aren't two separate things, or two separate stages on the journey. To be a Christian is to be a disciple. But then, secondly:

b. Each experience is different:

- Andrew and John are curious about Jesus and go to where he's making his home. That doesn't happen to anybody else.
- Peter gets renamed, but he's the only one.
- Philip gets called directly by Jesus: everybody in these stories takes the initiative to come to Jesus.
- Nathanael is skeptical, but then convinced by what is called "a word of knowledge." That too happens nowhere else.

This uniqueness is a deep mark of God's love for us. There are no cookie-cutter conversions. Each story is individually crafted and special to suit each unique child of God.

What do we learn?

1. I am encouraged to realize you don't need to know much to be an evangelist. These guys haven't known Jesus very long, and have only had one conversation with him—but they share what they know. Their

---

5. Jackson, "'If Necessary, Use Words.'"
6. Stetzer, "Call Yourself a Christian?" para. 6.

message is, "I may not be able to answer your questions, but I'll tell you what I know." That's powerful.

2. There have to be relationships of trust. Peter trusted his brother. It seems likely Philip knew and trusted Andrew and John. And Nathanael trusted Philip. Knowing isn't enough by itself: you can know someone well enough that you don't trust them! Sadly, that's true of some Christians. Their friends will trust them in everything except for talking about faith. One of the greatest compliments I was ever paid was by a young woman who invited her sister to an evangelistic Bible study I was leading. She said, "John is religious, but he's safe."

3. But then, there have to be things to invite people to—the equivalent of Jesus inviting Andrew and John back to where he was staying. This may be surprising, but we shouldn't assume the best place is the Sunday service, especially for those with no previous church experience, for whom it may just seem weird.

    Better to start by asking: Where in your experience does Jesus make his home? It may be a meal at your place, it may be a Sunday evening your small group does a barbecue for the neighbors, or it may be a group of Christians helping out in the community. We can invite people to experience Jesus wherever we know he makes his home.

4. The work of evangelism begins and ends with Jesus. Jesus takes the initiative with Andrew and John, and then with Philip. And only after that do they go and tell others—Peter and Nathanael. In each case, evangelism leads these guys back to Jesus. Evangelism is in the first place Jesus' work, and if we are his apprentices, this is one of the things he will teach us, if we ask.

35

Four Doors into Faith

This is one of three articles on evangelism commissioned by The Anglican, *the newspaper of the Anglican Diocese of Toronto, in 2012–2013.*

I was once in a parish where we were discussing evangelism, and after some time a very senior member of the congregation said very vehemently, "I have no intention of ever sharing the gospel with anybody!" This was not said in a way that invited rational discussion, and after an embarrassed silence the conversation moved on.

Had a response been possible, I think the best would have been, "Can you describe for us this gospel that you will never share?" The reason is that, as soon as you begin to articulate the gospel, it is clear why it is worth sharing. Even if it is as minimal as, "God loves you," it is still a revolutionary idea to those who have never heard it (and many have not). If it is a more robust summary of the good news than that—if we say, for example, God is at work in the world through Jesus Christ to renew and restore all things— the story becomes even more startling, and more shareable. But how do we then share it?

For most of this year, I have been meeting with a friend who is considering Christian faith. We have been doing what I think is one of the best things to do under those circumstances: we have been reading slowly through the gospel of Luke, and discussing who Jesus is—what he does and what he says, and what are the implications for our lives. Such an exercise is always a stretching and joyful one for me.

As we have got towards the end of Luke, however, Daniel and I have begun to talk about the way Jesus always prompts a response from people, and about what Daniel's response is going to be. That has prompted some new thoughts in me. One is that there are different ways people come to Christian faith. I think of them as four doors.

1. THE DOOR OF THE MIND

Some people become Christians simply through reading the Bible or another Christian book. You may have heard the story of a prisoner who found the thin paper of his Gideon New Testament perfect for rolling his cigarettes. He decided to read each page before he smoked it, and in this way smoked his way through Matthew, Mark, and Luke. When he came to John 3:16, however, he stopped as he was bowled over by the truth that "God so loved the world."

The story is told in so many different contexts (sometimes it is set in Northern Ireland, sometimes in Florida; and sometimes it is marijuana, not tobacco, that he smokes) that one wonders if it is apocryphal. But it is an illustration of something that certainly happens, even if the circumstances are not always so dramatic.

2. THE DOOR OF COMMUNITY

George started going to a church youth group simply because (in his opinion) they had the cutest girls in town. For a year, he proceeded to make life miserable for the youth leader, running intellectual rings around him, and causing other young people to doubt their faith. Then he had an encounter with God which turned him into a believer.

But, he says, unless he had become a part of the Christian community first—heard their prayers, seen the reality of faith in their eyes, seen the grace in their lives—it would never have happened. He belonged before he believed. Indeed, the belonging paved the way for the believing to happen.

3. THE DOOR OF ACTION

Some people behave themselves into belief. Jesus seems to be referring to this when he says, "Anyone who resolves to do the will of God will know whether the teaching is from God or whether I am speaking on my own" (John 7:17). In other words, if you try to do God's will, you will find out who Jesus really is. C. S. Lewis said he discovered this without intending to, that trying to be a good person, and failing, led him to faith in Jesus. Tongue in cheek, he warned others, "You must not do, you must not even try to do, the will of the Father unless you are prepared to 'know of the doctrine.'"[1]

Some time ago, I was told the story of a woman who decided to help out with a church's food bank. She herself claimed no faith or church allegiance, but she believed in what the food bank was trying to do. Over time, however, church friends working alongside her at the food bank noticed a change in her. Eventually, someone asked her, "You seem to consider yourself a Christian these days. Is that right?" And she replied with some embarrassment, "I guess I do!" Behaving—and belonging—led to believing.

4. THE DOOR OF MIRACLE

Evangelism is always the work of God, whichever door is involved, but seldom is that as clear as when people come to faith through the door of miracle.

Frequently, these experiences happen to people in non-Western cultures, perhaps because they tend to have a more holistic view of the spiritual life. It is not uncommon for them to see a vision or have a dream of Jesus, and begin to worship and follow him, before ever reading the Bible or joining a church.

However, these events are more common, even in the West, than we realize. One priest friend, in her first year at Trinity College, thought of herself as a seeker, and checked out many churches, to no avail. Then one day she walked into the Trinity chapel and was overwhelmed by the reality of God. Roughly 20 percent in mainline denominations claim to have had this kind of Damascus Road experience, and just over one-third in evangelical denominations. Who knew?

We used to assume people had to figure out what they believed, and then they would show up at church, get baptized, and start joining in the life of the church. They would believe, and then they would belong and begin to behave like followers of Jesus.

---

1. Lewis, *Surprised by Joy*, 213.

In recent years, however, we have realized it's not that simple, and certainly not that linear, in the lives of most who come to faith as adults. Any or all of those four things may be involved. Any one of the four may be the starting point—the door in—and the other doors will simply lead deeper into faith.

If we want to share the good news of what God is doing in our world, we need to be sensitive to this diversity. Churches can actually be helpful in opening at least the first three doors—giving people opportunities to learn about Christian faith (believing), providing a welcoming community where people can get a sense of the life of faith (belonging), and offering new people an opportunity to join in various avenues for service (behaving). The fourth door, unfortunately—or perhaps it is just as well—is outside our control!

Daniel and I have talked about which might be the door for him. He has grown in his understanding of what it means to be an apprentice of Jesus: the mind door. He has lots of Christian friends, and knows the reality of their faith: the community door. And he has begun to volunteer at a downtown Christian ministry: the action door. Might the next be the miracle door? We shall have to wait and see.

36

Are Evangelists Born or Made?

TEACHING EVANGELISM IS AN *awkward business. I used to complain that, if I were Professor of Church History or Systematic Theology, or several other things, nobody would care what I did in my spare time. Even if I were Professor of Preaching, it wouldn't matter greatly how often I actually preached. But with evangelism, well, it comes with the expectation that the teacher would do evangelism, at least sometimes. The same was true with giving the students assignments. I can practice preaching in the preaching class, and it's pretty much the real thing. But practicing evangelism in class? There's not much similarity.*

For a few years, I would send the students out with a questionnaire, stopping people around the campus and asking them their views on religion, and probing their understanding of Christian faith. This had some merit, taught nondefensive listening, and caused some useful learning. But I came to feel it was rather manipulative, because the main reason we were doing the survey was to engage people in conversation, not really to collect and tabulate their views. This article, from Good Idea! *in June 2013, describes the most satisfactory solution I came up with.*

Some people just seem to be natural evangelists. They talk about faith freely and people respond with equal freedom. Some of them don't know they're evangelists, and would deny it vehemently. Personally, I try not to tell them.

My philosophy is: just let them get on with it, and don't mess with their heads. Worst-case scenario: they read books about evangelism, take courses on it, learn strategies and techniques, and end up quite ineffective. Why waste such a valuable and rare resource?

Other natural evangelists are OK with the word, but don't seem inhibited or pretentious about it. I remember one friend (an Anglican priest, as it happens) who was being interviewed by a police officer about a crime he had witnessed. Early on in the conversation, the officer asked, "And what do you do for a living, sir?"

To which Roger replied, "I'm an evangelist. Do you know what an evangelist is?"

It was an hour later when they finally got to talking about the crime.

But what about the rest of us? Is there hope for us? Can we be trained to do something that (apparently) doesn't come naturally? Well, it certainly happens in many other areas of life. Not many of us are born with strong instincts about how to drive a car, after all, but most of us are sufficiently motivated that we manage to learn this unnatural skill so it becomes, well, second nature.

Of course, there is training and then there is training. I sometimes show my students a book called *Soul Winning Made Easy*, by C. S. Lovett (not to be confused with anyone else with those initials). Lovett is clear that evangelism can be very simply learned if one follows his steps. For example, you can say to your "prospect":

> "If it's all right with you, I'd like to read you four verses of Scripture and explain them to you . . . That would be okay, wouldn't it?" (Nod your head affirmatively.) Note: Man is a suggestible being . . . . A simple nod of your head has the power to activate your request. He'll find himself answering you automatically. "Go ahead," or "Sure."[1]

There must be a better way, surely? I have struggled with this question because of my classroom teaching of evangelism. Obviously, evangelism cannot be learned simply by classroom lectures and discussion. But on the one hand, I don't want to send students out onto the streets to buttonhole unsuspecting passersby with an approach of the "I'd like to read you four verses of Scripture" variety. But it seems equally wrong to say, "Try and make a friend, and by the end of term, share the gospel with them and see if they become a Christian." What kind of friendship is that?

---

1. Lovett, *Soul-Winning Made Easy*, 53–54.

This past semester, I found one kind of solution to my dilemma. I handed out to students in my basic evangelism class a four-part study on the Gospel of Luke (one parable, one miracle, the crucifixion, and a resurrection story), and asked them to find a friend who did not profess Christian faith, to see if they would be interested in four weekly discussions on the biography of Jesus, each one to last no more than half an hour. To the students' amazement, only one met with a refusal.

The experiences they had were varied and eye-opening. More than one commented, "My friend saw things in the passage that I had never seen." One student who lives in a house with other guys invited one of them to study at the kitchen table, and was taken aback when the others wanted to join in too. Several were surprised when the four sessions were over, and their friend wanted to do more. One friend said it was the first time her religious views had been taken seriously. Most of the studies went well over the half hour. One student reported in class, "I never knew evangelism could be so much fun!"

What made this such a good experience? The students learned that (1) people in general are not averse to this kind of discussion; (2) evangelism is a process that takes time; (3) it does not require preaching, shouting, manipulation, proof-texting, being an apologetics expert, or even nodding; (4) the best evangelism is relational—just as the gospel itself is at its heart relational; (5) nothing is better in evangelism than helping people encounter Jesus in the pages of Scripture; and (6) God gives us joy when we share the gospel.

Of course, there are few worthwhile things that can be learned in one go like that (think driving a car). This experience won't benefit the students much unless it inspires them to do the same again and again. And again. Not necessarily using those studies on Luke, of course (though that wouldn't be bad), but applying those same six principles.

The problem, I find, is simply doing it. There are at least two reasons it is difficult to practice (in both senses) evangelism. One is that, particularly for those in busy local church ministry, those who are already Christians can suck up 100 percent (and more) of one's time, so that none is left for the outsider.

The other is rather deeper: we instinctively avoid situations where we are vulnerable to hurt and rejection, where we are not in control, and where we don't know the outcome. And all those things describe evangelism! This means it takes a deliberate, God-empowered choice to deny that instinct—"Lord, give me courage as I go to the coffee shop and see who's there"; "Holy Spirit, go before me as I ask my friend if she would like to do that Bible study with me"; "God, give me the words to ask my neighbor to our special

Mother's Day service." Often we find ways to avoid that prayer and that choice—and "I'm too busy" is certainly one of my personal favorites.

Having said that, I am encouraged by Jesus' words: "I will make you fish for people" (Mark 1:17). Jesus is willing to teach us to evangelize (as he will with everything we need for our discipleship). I know in my case it is taking a long time, but he is very patient—and I like to think that, little by little, I am learning. The question is not whether he is willing to teach us: it is only a question of how far we are willing to learn.

37

How Does Evangelism Happen?

A Study in Teamwork

I HAVE PROBABLY WRITTEN *more about evangelism than about any other topic over the years. There is a certain irony about this, because I am not a strongly gifted evangelist and covet the abilities of those who are. As a result, I am haunted by the words of the Epistle of James: "Not many of you should become teachers, my brothers and sisters, for you know that we who teach will be judged with greater strictness" (James 3:1). But then evangelistic opportunities are dropped in my lap, like the one described here. This was published in* The Anglican *newspaper in 2009.*

Duncan was, I suppose you might say, a seeker. When he arrived in Toronto as a graduate student that Fall, he was looking for something or someone to help him understand Christianity. Then, through a succession of links, he got in touch with me. Could we meet and talk?

We met in a university coffee shop. After the preliminaries, he asked, "So, if I become a Christian, will I have to vote Conservative for the rest of my life?" I've had lots of this kind of conversation over the years, but I confess that was a new opening line.

Over the weeks that followed, we talked about many of his questions—the historical basis for Christianity, the reputation of the church in the world, and not least what it might mean for Duncan to live as a follower of Jesus (including, of course, how he might vote). Then, some time before Christmas, he emailed me in the middle of the week to say, "I've opened my heart to God in the way that we've talked about. I didn't expect to feel different, but actually I do—I feel more alive than I've ever felt before."

From that point on, our weekly conversations over coffee took a new turn. In particular, we began to read the Gospels with a new intensity—two students of Jesus trying to learn from our teacher. The first time we did this, to my surprise, Duncan brought a Bible with him. I didn't even know he owned a Bible. Out of idle curiosity, I pulled it across the table toward me, and opened the front cover. There I read, "To Duncan, from Dave." It was dated a few years earlier. "Who's Dave?" I asked.

"Oh, Dave was my best friend in high school," he replied. "He was a Christian, and we had lots of discussions about faith over the years. But he never managed to persuade me. Then, when we graduated, he gave me this."

Our Bible studies continued through the school year. They were lively, intriguing, edgy, and often humorous. As the spring drew on, he said one day, "By the way, I have a friend coming to see me at the end of term. I'd like you to meet her."

"Who's that?" I asked.

"Meredith and I dated through university," he replied. "She was a Christian. Towards the end of our undergraduate years, I asked her if she would marry me. She told me she couldn't marry someone who wasn't a Christian. At the time, I thought, what is this fascist religion where you can't marry whoever you want?" Duncan smiled ruefully. "Now I understand perfectly."

So one fine May morning, I was introduced to Meredith. And, as I shook her hand, I smiled and said, "Nice to be on the same team as you." Because I was.

So who was the evangelist in Duncan's life? Me? Well, in a way I suppose so. Certainly I was the person who just happened to be around when he decided he wanted to be a follower of Jesus. Maybe our discussions were the final nudge he needed. I don't really know. But I do know Jesus several times spoke of the work of the kingdom (of which evangelism is a part) like farming—a process with several stages, from sowing to reaping, all of them overseen by God. Paul understands this principle when he writes, "I sowed, Apollos watered, but God gave the increase."

So in Duncan's case I was the reaper. But, of course, I could not have done what I did unless Dave had sowed the seed and Meredith had watered that seed. It was almost as though Jesus had me in mind when he said (also in the context of evangelism), "Others have labored and you have entered into their labor."

I sometimes wonder how Dave felt when he and Duncan parted ways after high school. He had certainly "labored" to be a good witness, but I think in his place I would have felt discouraged: "I had so hoped that Duncan would become a Christian, but he didn't. If only I had been smarter, prayed more, been a better friend. Maybe that Bible will help him, if he reads it." I wonder if Meredith felt the same. Each of them knew him for three years. Over that time, they bore consistent daily witness, by their lives and (as opportunity offered) by their words. I, by contrast, knew Duncan for three months. Frankly, I had the easy job, the fun job—for me, anyway, pure joy.

But God, who oversees the whole process of evangelism, used all of us in different ways to help Duncan move to become a follower of Jesus. The work of evangelism is the work of the whole body of Christ. And when people finally become Christians, then, as Jesus knew, "sower and reaper . . . rejoice together" (John 4:36).

38

The Way I See it: Believing is Seeing

I knew Louise as a student at Carleton University in the 1980s. She was a member of the InterVarsity group there where I was IVCF staff. Occasionally a group of students would go to a movie together, and on one occasion, I went too, and sat next to Louise. I don't know what the movie was (I have a feeling it might have been Lawrence of Arabia*), but the experience of providing a commentary for a visually impaired person was deeply thought provoking.*

Over the years, one of the ideas that has impacted me most deeply has been that of Christianity as a worldview, a view of the world, a way of looking at things, that has light to shed on every aspect. I learned this first from Brian Walsh and Richard Middleton in the 1970s, but since then I have taught worldview many times myself. My experience at the movie with Louise encapsulated the idea of worldview in a single powerful, succinct—and visual—metaphor.

This article appeared in Christian Week *newspaper in the spring of 2008.*

Going to a movie with Louise is an experience. She absolutely loves movies. But there are some problems. First, there's the dog. Where does he sit, or lie? Does he prefer his popcorn with or without butter? But mostly there is the constant need for a running commentary.

"Why are they laughing?"

"It's just the expression on her face."

"Now he's getting his gun out."
"She looks as if she's going to explode."
"They're all watching the sky."
Louise, of course, is blind.

Seeing is absolutely fundamental to the experience of most of us. In the movie, we understand the significance of the raised eyebrow, the glowering red sky, the sign saying "Enter at your own risk." It is all lost on Louise.

Believing in God has to do with seeing too. I talked to David recently. As we looked out over a lovely winter landscape, he shook his head.

"Why can't everyone see God in that?"
"Did you always see God?" I asked.
"No," he replied.
"What came first—believing or seeing?"
He thought for a minute.

"I think I believed a bit, and then I could see a bit, then I believed some more, and I could see some more. And now I see it all, all the time."

The scientist sounds skeptical when believers say believing comes before seeing. Surely we should only believe what we see? But even scientists don't always follow that rule. Often advances come because a scientist has a flash of insight into a problem. She believes she has found the answer, rushes to the lab to try it out, and discovers what she believed actually is the case: it can be seen. Believing first, seeing afterwards. Of course, that kind of believing is itself a kind of seeing, a vision, an insight, but not physical seeing; rather, seeing with the eyes of faith.

After one of the debates I did with a philosophy professor on the existence of God, I began thinking about the friend I had debated with. He lives in precisely the same world I inhabit. We walk the same university corridors, exchange greetings with the same people, eat in the same restaurants, and order from the same menu. But all the time, we see things differently. I see God everywhere in my world. I look for God in the lives of the people I meet. I thank God for providing my food. My friend does none of those things. They seem to him bizarre and inappropriate, even neurotic.

To say people are "spiritually blind" is not an interesting theological theory. It is not the rash overstatement of a zealous evangelist. It is an observable reality. People simply do not see God, where to the believer God is clearly standing and beckoning. They do not believe in God, so they cannot see God.

The 1989 movie, *Honey, I Shrunk the Kids*, is not exactly Oscar material. But it did say a lot about seeing and believing. Rick Moranis plays the father, an eccentric scientist, who really does shrink his kids—and then by accident sweeps them up and puts them out with the garbage. Before he figures out what has happened, they have begun to make their way painfully, slowly, through the immense jungle of the backyard, to their house.

When realization dawns, Moranis takes perfectly logical action: he arranges a system whereby he and his wife are suspended from a thing like a rotary clothes line, and scan the ground from a distance of three feet or so with binoculars, trying to spot their microscopic children. The neighbors decide the scientist and his wife are totally out of their tree—and so by any "normal" standards they are—but to us, the viewers, their actions make perfect sense. We, and they, know there is a whole world, invisible to full-size people, which needs to be treated with utmost seriousness and care.

The way believers live is equally eccentric to the agnostic or atheist. Their lifestyle—actions, attitudes, priorities—makes sense only when you understand they live in the light of a world that is totally invisible to the untrained eye. Then it becomes utterly logical. Believers know something, see something the unbeliever does not. But how do you help someone see what they cannot see?

In a recent discussion on the existence of God with some philosophy students, I showed them a picture, a *trompe l'oeil*. You may have seen it. Looked at in one way, it is the picture of an old woman's face. But many people see it as the picture of a young woman's face.

"Who sees a young woman?" I asked. "An old woman? Both?"

The class was split three ways. The interesting thing then was to see those who saw both trying to help those who saw only one. The most helpful tool was the index finger.

"Look," they said. "Don't you see how the old woman's mouth can be the young woman's choker?"

Philosophy seemed to have gone out of the window. They were learning to see.

Finally, they all got it. But it was hard. Peer pressure certainly helped. "How come all these other people see a young woman and I only see an old woman? Am I stupid or something?" Imaginative effort helped too: "Try to think of the nose on your old woman as a chin." Sounds strange, but it is the only way. And eventually, for all of them, there came the moment of illumination, the moment when they said, "Aha! I see." They believed their friends were probably right—that it was not a conspiracy to make fools of them—and eventually their believing led to seeing.

The movie gives another clue. The apparently eccentric couple explain to their skeptical neighbors what has happened—by now to the neighbors' children as well as to their own—and little by little the neighbors come to believe it must be true—because, bizarre though it sounds, it is the only explanation which makes sense of everything that has happened.

So how do people get to see? They have to be convinced that those who say they see are not totally crazy. They have to understand how this new explanation actually makes more sense of things, in spite of its unfamiliarity. They have to be told, little by little, how the world appears once you have this new way of seeing. And, most importantly, they have to want to see, in spite of the cost. Unlike physical blindness, this kind of blindness is to do with choice.

Another word for helping people to see spiritually is "evangelism"; living consistently in the light of a world they do not see, so that they begin to feel its reality even before they see it; talking about the way the world appears to believing eyes; explaining what we see in the movie called life. Until, perhaps long after, they say, "Now I see for myself what you meant."

39

Will They Come Back Next Week?

The Challenge of Preaching at Christmas

THERE ARE PREACHERS WHO *plow on with their weekly sermons through the lectionary, whatever the time of year, and regardless of who might be visiting the congregation. The philosophy seems to be, "If those people are not here every Sunday, of course they will feel excluded. The remedy is in their own hands." Or maybe the underlying assumption is all visitors are of course thoroughly churched people, and don't need anyone to make allowances for them. The irony is, often these are churches which consider themselves to be inclusive in other more obvious ways, but are blind to the need of visitors to be included. My contribution to* Good Idea! *in the fall of 2015 was to address this issue.*

Apparently, it's just one of those long-standing Christmas traditions. More people will come to services at Christmas than at any other time of year. And the majority of those people will not come back for another twelve months. Is this inevitable? Do we simply shrug and accept it as a sad reality? Or is there something we can do to make those people think it might be worthwhile to come back sooner than next Christmas—maybe even next week?

Some of the answers are obvious, though not always easy: a genuinely welcoming community; liturgy that is done well; music that delights the ear and the heart; and quality refreshments afterwards, for a start. All those require the enthusiastic cooperation of the church community. But I want to address another component of the service that is primarily the responsibility of one person: the sermon.

How do we preach at Christmas in such a way that the hearers say, "Wow! That's amazing. Maybe I need to come back and hear more," instead of, "Ah yes, the boring sermon. Another reason I gave up on church twenty years ago. I remember it so well." Here are some modest suggestions:

1. Name people's hang-ups—whether or not we share them

Many people outside the church assume churchfolk do not think like them, and certainly don't understand the doubts and reservations they experience around church stuff. To name those things helps people relax: "Wow, the preacher knows how I think, and seems to think it's normal!"

What should we name? Here are just a few:

- Difficulties with the historicity of the story: "Many of us have a hard time believing things happened just the way they're described in the story."
- Difficulties with adult belief: "We think the Christmas story is OK for kids, but not for adults."
- Difficulties with church: "Many people have had bad experiences with church, and that's deeply sad."
- Difficulties with the incarnation: "To say 'he came down to earth from heaven' makes it sound as though Jesus was an alien being visiting from another planet."
- Difficulties with faith: Mark Twain said, "Faith is believing what you know ain't true."

Of course, we can go on to address whatever the problem is, but we need to start by naming it as a legitimate concern. Otherwise the hearers are always thinking, "Ah, but if you knew my particular questions, my doubts, my experience, you'd understand why I'm not here more often." If we can disarm those reservations, it increases the likelihood that our hearers can hear the good news.

2. Speak from the heart—and take time to find it

John Stott says somewhere that, although he loved to preach the atonement and did so frequently, he was careful not to use clichés in doing do. Each time, he would seek to be personally reminded of the reality of the cross, and to find fresh ways of talking about it that would engage both him and his hearers.

The same is true for the incarnation (and, I suppose, ideally for all Christian truth). I would suggest our sermon preparation is not complete until we ourselves have been touched afresh by the reality of God become a human being, until we feel the utter goodness of the good news, and our sermon-in-the-making is more than words. "Out of the abundance of the heart the mouth speaks," says Jesus (Luke 6:45). Let's make sure our hearts are full to overflowing before we speak. People recognize authenticity, and they recognize when we are just saying the words without feeling them.

3. Avoid theological jargon

C. S. Lewis says there is a place for in-house technical language in every profession or social group. We can't manage without it: it can be precise and efficient. Once we step outside that specialized community, however, our language has to change. In particular, explanations tend to take far longer. Lewis suggests most in-house words require ten everyday words in order to explain them. He adds if your job is to communicate with outsiders—especially in the name of Christ—then suck it up (I paraphrase): take that extra time, and don't grudge it; use those ten words (unfamiliar though they may be in church), and don't look for short cuts.[1] For example:

- Talk about "the author writing himself into the script of the play" rather than "the incarnation"—this is a C. S. Lewis analogy (ten words instead of two).

- Talk about "Matthew's biography of Jesus" rather than "the Gospel of Matthew"—it's not obvious to an unchurched person what "a gospel" is.

- Talk about "the story" rather than "the text" or "the narrative." Avoid academic terms, unless your congregation attracts a lot of university folk, of course.

This kind of translation is actually a good discipline for us. Apart from anything else, it's what missionaries have always done.

---

1. Lewis, "Before We can Communicate," 255–56.

4. Do something surprising—even if it's outside our comfort zone

We live in a multimedia age. Sadly, for those of us over a certain age at least, words alone seldom stick in the memory. Our sermon is far more likely to be remembered and discussed over Christmas lunch if it is more than words. Why not consider things like:

- Having a roving microphone in the congregation. Ask questions that invite a one- or two-word answer. "What comes to your mind when you think of Christmas?" is simple and sure to get people involved. Don't ask for stories or you might never get your microphone back.
- Preaching from the aisle rather than the pulpit. People in the Western hemisphere feel (perhaps since the 1960s) that informal equals sincere, and formal equals inauthentic. There is really no rational basis for it, but it's worth remembering.
- Having a new Christian say (briefly) how his or her view of Christmas has changed. A personal story from an amateur can carry more weight than the views of the professional.
- Including a short dramatic sketch on the subject of the sermon. (As I write this, I remember one such at Trinity Anglican Church in Streetsville [Ontario], over ten years ago. Even now I find it moving.)
- If you have the technology, showing an appropriate video clip. The website textweek.com has a tab called "movie index," which offers lots of good ideas.

And if some of these suggestions seem somehow beneath our dignity, let's remember this is, after all, the festival of the humiliation of the Word.

5. Show how the gospel makes a difference

Postmodern people don't care whether Christianity is true, but they are interested to know whether it works. It's a legitimate question. After all, it is "by their fruits"—not by their compelling arguments—that "you will know them."

So how might it affect our hearers' lives if they believed God really became a human being? How might the most amazing event in history cause them to see the world differently? How might they treat their spouse, their colleagues, their in-laws, their neighbors, differently? How might leisure or work or sex seem different? How might life be more joyful? And, to be honest, how might life be more difficult? (There is always a cost to believing).

Of course, it will help if we can say too how the incarnation (forgive the technical term) has changed—and is changing—the way we and our congregation live.

SACRAMENTAL PREACHING

Preaching at Christmas is a challenge, but one worthy of the season. After all, if we believe "the Word became flesh and dwelt among us," (John 1:14) the sermon can be a sacrament of that same incarnation—not just talking about God, but by our preaching giving the hearers a taste of the God who enters our world, who participates in our language and our culture, who speaks to us right where we are, to affirm us and challenge us at the depths of our being.

Whether our guests actually come back the week after Christmas is their responsibility before God, not ours. Our responsibility is to be faithful in representing the gospel as best we can—and then to leave the rest to the God who loves them enough to come to earth for them.

40

O Come, O Come, Emmanuel

Liturgy and Evangelism

THIS CHAPTER WAS ANOTHER Good Idea! *article, also just before Christmas, this time in 2014. It was written just after the event it describes, and for me was a lovely illustration of how the liturgical and evangelistic impulses of the church are not really at odds with one another, but are complementary in pointing to Christ and inviting us to trust him.*

I was on sabbatical recently. Well, OK, not a real sabbatical. It was only four hours long. It was actually something called a "Brown Bag Sabbatical," because you bring your own lunch. A very simple idea. And yet that mini-sabbath served the same purpose as a longer sabbatical: refreshment, fresh ideas, and (as of this moment) writing.

The day was led by Sister Constance Joanna from the Sisters of St. John the Divine in Willowdale, in the north of Toronto, and she introduced us to the "O antiphons." That may be an unfamiliar term, but if you have ever sung "O come, O come, Emmanuel" at this time of year, you are in fact already familiar with the O antiphons, since the hymn is based directly on them.

OBSCURE LITURGICAL TRIVIA?

The O antiphons probably came into being in monasteries of the early church and were used widely by the eighth century, as a way of preparing for Christmas. An antiphon is the short piece of choral music sung immediately before and after each psalm and canticle, often a single sentence, to introduce and then to reinforce the theme of the psalm. The O antiphons were just such pieces, one for each of the seven days leading up to Christmas Day, and sung at evening prayer before and after the Magnificat, Mary's hymn of thanksgiving in Luke 1. And the "O?" Quite simple, really: each one begins with an "O."

So why is this more than an obscure piece of liturgical trivia, useless in our more streamlined, high-tech world? And how on earth might it have anything to do with evangelism?

Listen first to what the antiphons say:

1. O Wisdom, from the mouth of the Most High, you reign over all things to the ends of the earth: come and teach us how to live.

2. O Lord, and head of the house of Israel, you appeared to Moses in the fire of the burning bush and you gave the law on Sinai: come with outstretched arm and ransom us.

3. O Branch of Jesse, standing as a sign among the nations, all kings will keep silence before you and all peoples will summon you to their aid: come, set us free and delay no more.

4. O Key of David and scepter of the house of Israel, you open and none can shut; you shut and none can open: come and free the captives from prison.

5. O Morning Star, splendor of the light eternal and bright Sun of righteousness: come and enlighten all who dwell in darkness and in the shadow of death.

6. O King of the nations, you alone can fulfill their desires: Cornerstone, you make opposing nations one: come and save the creature you fashioned from clay.

7. O Emmanuel, hope of the nations and their Savior: come and save us, Lord our God.

Three aspects relate to evangelism:

THE O ANTIPHONS SPEAK OF JESUS

First, each antiphon focuses on a characteristic of Jesus Christ: he is Wisdom, he is Lord, he is Branch of Jesse, he is the Key of David, he is the Morning Star, and he is Emmanuel.

Evangelism, whether in conversation or in preaching, is not in the first place about trying to prove the existence of God, or wrestling with the problem of evil. In the first place, it is helping people see what Jesus is like. And this is what he is like.

One Muslim convert to Christianity saw the implications of this, perhaps more clearly than long-term Christians do, when he said:

> I am a Christian for one reason alone—the absolute worshipability of Jesus Christ. By that word, I mean that I have found no other being in the universe who compels my adoration as he has done.[1]

The Jesus of the O antiphons is supremely worshipable. Our brown bag meditation on the Os reminded me of this truth.

THE O ANTIPHONS REMIND US OF THE WHOLE STORY

Second, the whole of the Christian story is told in the O antiphons. They begin with Jesus as Wisdom, the agency of creation (Prov 8:22–31). The next three speak of God's calling of the people of Israel. He is their Lord, who called them, sought to teach them the law, and set them free from captivity. Then Jesus is the "branch of Jesse," a king descended from David and destined to rule over the world in righteousness. And this same king is the "key" of David, with power and compassion able to set the captives free.

The last three speak of Jesus more directly. He is the Morning Star, the first sign of the dawning of God's new creation. He is King of the nations, in submission to whose rule is found world peace. And finally—the climax of the seven—Jesus is Emmanuel, God with us.

These days, we often speak of "the Christian story" instead of "the Christian faith." And conversion is not so much "accepting the faith" as "allowing God to work my story into his Big Story." It's a very useful metaphor.

But what is that Big Story? The Os remind us: it is a story of a good world gone wrong, the story of a creator who takes upon his shoulders the responsibility of putting things right—even at the cost of his own life. God's story is about the Spirit of Jesus at work in the world, drawing men and

---

1. Warren, *I Believe in the Great Commission*, 152.

women together into a new community of apprentices who work with God toward the renewal of all things. And it is a story with the ultimate happy ending, when all wrongs are put right, God brings down the curtain on this story, and a new one opens.

Evangelism is not talking about the forgiveness of sins, or discovering meaning in life, or finding hope beyond the grave, in isolation from the telling of the whole story. Sin only makes sense if this is God's good world which we have messed up. Meaning in life can't be divorced from the purposes of God in the world. And the resurrection is not just a guarantee of life after death, but the turning point in God's bringing about a whole new creation. The O antiphons remind us of this big picture.

THE O ANTIPHONS AND THE LOGIC OF PRAYER

Finally, the O antiphons speak of prayer. Each one begins with "O," but each one includes a "come": come and teach us how to live; come with outstretched arm and ransom us; come set us free and delay no more; come and free the captives from prison; come and enlighten all who dwell in darkness and in the shadow of death; come and save the creature you fashioned from clay; come and save us, Lord our God.

I confess, when I teach about evangelism, I don't say enough about prayer. But my hunch is most people don't come to faith unless someone is praying for them. And what is conversion to Christ except learning to pray: Lord, please accept me; Lord, forgive me; Lord, take my life. The Os remind me that once I realize who Jesus is, I cannot help but see my neediness, and that in turn leads me to prayer.

I have a fancy definition of evangelism I teach to students, but someone recently suggested a much simpler one: "Evangelism is overflow." And that's right. Overflow of awareness of the majesty of Jesus Christ. Overflow of wonder at the big story the love of God is writing about this world. And overflow of prayer, both praise and petition, to this same God made known to us in Jesus Christ. They're all there, in the O antiphons of Advent.

O come, O come, Emmanuel.

Bibliography

Appleby, George, ed. *The Oxford Book of Prayer*. Oxford: Oxford University Press, 1985.

Augustine. "Homily VII." www.ccel.org/ccel/schaff/npnf107.iv.x.html.

Bowen, John P. *Growing Up Christian: Why Young People Stay in Church, Leave Church and (Sometimes) Come Back to Church*. Vancouver: Regent College Press, 2010.

Brauer, Jerald C., ed. *The Westminster Dictionary of Church History*. Philadelphia: Westminster, 1971.

Brow, Robert. *"Go Make Learners": A New Model for Discipleship in the Church*. Wheaton, IL: Harold Shaw, 1981.

Brown, D. W. "Pietism." In *New Dictionary of Theology*, edited by Sinclair Ferguson et al., 515–17. Downers Grove, IL: InterVarsity, 1988.

Burbridge, Paul, and Murray Watts. *Lightning Sketches*. London: Hodder and Stoughton, 1981.

Calvin, John. *Hebrews and 1 and 2 Peter*. Grand Rapids: Eerdmans, 1963.

———. *Institutes of the Christian Religion*. 2 vols. Philadelphia: Westminster, 1960.

Campolo, Tony. "If I Had to Live it Over Again." https://soundcloud.com/tonycampolo/if-i-had-to-live-it-over-again.

Caraman, Philip. *Ignatius Loyola: A Biography of the Founder of the Jesuits*. San Francisco: Harper and Row, 1990.

Carroll, Lewis. *The Annotated Alice: Alice's Adventures in Wonderland and Through the Looking Glass*. Edited by Martin Gardner. Cleveland: Forum, 1970.

Common Praise. Toronto: Anglican Book Centre, 1998.

Corrie, G. E., ed. *Certain Sermons, Appointed by the Queen's Majesty to Be . . . Read by All Parsons, Vicars, and Curates . . . in Their Churches . . . Newly Imprinted in Parts According as is Mentioned in the Book of Common Prayers, 1574*. Cambridge: Parker, 1850.

Crouch, Andy. *Strong and Weak: Embracing a Life of Love, Risk and True Flourishing*. Downers Grove, IL: InterVarsity, 2016.

Ferguson, Sinclair, et al., eds. *New Dictionary of Theology*. Downers Grove, IL: InterVarsity, 1988.

Forster, Marc, dir. *Stranger than Fiction*. 2006; Culver City, CA: Columbia Pictures, 2006.

Foster, Richard. *Streams of Living Water: Celebrating the Great Traditions of Christ*. New York: HarperCollins, 2001.

Goleman, Daniel, "Long-Married Couples Do Look Alike, Study Finds." *The New York Times*, Aug. 11, 1987. https://www.nytimes.com/1987/08/11/science/long-married-couples-do-look-alike-study-finds.html.

Grabiec, Christopher M. "Time for a Christian Truce." *The Niagara Anglican*, June 2008. https://niagaraanglican.ca/newspaper/docs/2008/june.pdf

Griffiths, Michael. *Cinderella with Amnesia: A Practical Discussion of the Relevance of the Church*. London: InterVarsity, 1975. Reprinted as *Missional Body: The Beauty and Purpose of the Church*. Allen TX: Bold Grace, 2019.

Herbert, George. *The Country Parson: His Character and Rule of Holy Life*. Mahwah, NJ: Paulist, 1981.

Ignatius of Loyola. *Letters of St. Ignatius of Loyola*. Chicago: Loyola, 1959.

Jackson, Jack. "'If Necessary, Use Words': Really?" http://institute.wycliffecollege.ca/2015/09/if-necessary-use-words-really.

Haystack Bible Commentary. "Jer 2:13: 'For My People Have Committed Two Evils: They Have Forsaken Me, the Fountain of Living Waters, to Hew for Themselves Cisterns, Broken Cisterns That Can Hold No Water.'" http://haystackbiblecommentary.blogspot.com/2014/05/jer-213-for-my-people-have-committed.html.

Kierkegaard, Soren. *Journals IV*. Princeton: Princeton University Press, 2011.

Lewis, C. S. "Before We can Communicate." In *God in the Dock: Essays on Theology and Ethics*, edited by Walter Hooper, 254–57. Grand Rapids: Eerdmans, 1970.

———. "Cross Examination." In *God in the Dock: Essays on Theology and Ethics*, edited by Walter Hooper, 258–67. Grand Rapids: Eerdmans, 1970.

———. *The Four Loves*. London: Collins Fount, 1977.

———. *The Great Divorce*. New York: HarperCollins, 2001.

———. *A Grief Observed*. London: Faber and Faber, 1961.

———. *The Last Battle*. London: Fontana, 1980.

———. *Miracles*. London: Fontana, 1976.

———. *Prince Caspian*. Harmondsworth, UK: Puffin, 1979.

———. "Rejoinder to Dr. Pittenger." In *God in the Dock*, edited by Walter Hooper, 177–83. Grand Rapids: Eerdmans, 1970.

———. *Surprised by Joy*. London: Geoffrey Bles, 1955.

———. "The World's Last Night." In *Fernseeds and Elephants*, edited by Walter Hooper, 50-68. London: HarperCollins 1975.

Lovett, C. S. *Soul-Winning Made Easy*. Baldwin Park, CA: Personal Christianity, 1981.

Mencken, H. L. *A Mencken Chrestomathy: His Own Selection of His Choicest Writing*. New York: Knopf Doubleday, 2012.

Milton, John. *Paradise Lost*. Indianapolis: Hackett, 2003.

Mouw, Richard. *He Shines in All That's Fair*. Grand Rapids: Eerdmans, 2001.

Newbigin, Lesslie. *The Gospel in a Pluralist Society*. Grand Rapids: Eerdmans, 1989.

Peck, M. Scott. *The Road Less Traveled: A New Psychology of Love, Traditional Values and Spiritual Growth*. New York: Touchstone, 1978.

Peter, Laurence, and Raymond Hull. *The Peter Principle: Why Things Always Go Wrong*. New York: William Morrow, 1969.

Pippert, Rebecca Manley. *Out of the Saltshaker*. Downers Grove, IL: InterVarsity, 1979.

Pountney, Michael James. *Michael's Page*. Victoria, BC: Friesen, 2020.
Power, Thomas, ed. *Confronting the Idols of Our Age*. Eugene, OR: Wipf & Stock, 2017.
Purcell, Mary. *The First Jesuit: St. Ignatius Loyola*. New York: Image, 1965.
Ratzinger, Joseph. *Introduction to Christianity*. San Francisco: Ignatius, 2010.
Sayers, Dorothy. *The Man Born to be King*. London: Gollancz, 1943.
Shortt, Rupert. *Rowan's Rule: The Biography of the Archbishop of Canterbury*. Grand Rapids: Eerdmans, 2008.
Smail, Thomas. *Reflected Glory*. London: Hodder and Stoughton, 1975.
Solzhenitsyn, Aleksandr I. *The Gulag Archipelago Two*. New York: Harper and Row, 1975.
Southey, Robert. *A Life of John Wesley*. London: Hutchinson, 1820.
Stackhouse, Reginald. "Church Planting in the 1950s: A Historical Perspective." In *Green Shoots Out of Dry Ground: Growing a New Future for the Church in Canada*, edited by John P. Bowen, 35–41. Eugene, OR: Wipf & Stock, 2013.
Stetzer, Ed. "Call Yourself a Christian? Start Talking about Jesus Christ." *The Washington Post*, May 19, 2016. https://www.washingtonpost.com/news/acts-of-faith/wp/2016/05/19/call-yourself-a-christian-start-talking-about-jesus-christ/?noredirect=on&utm_term=.a41ebf22f33b.
Stevens, R. Paul. *The Other Six Days: Vocation, Work, and Ministry in Biblical Perspective*. Grand Rapids: Eerdmans, 2000.
Stott, John R. W. *Christian Mission in the Modern World*. Downers Grove, IL: InterVarsity, 1975.
———. "I Believe in the Church of England." In *Authentic Christianity from the Writings of John Stott*, edited by Timothy Dudley-Smith, 309–10. Downers Grove, IL: InterVarsity, 1995.
———. *What is an Evangelical?* London: Falcon, 1977.
Temple, William. *Readings in John's Gospel*. London: MacMillan, 1945.
Templeton, Charles. *Farewell to God: My Reasons for Rejecting the Christian Faith*. Toronto: McClelland and Stewart, 1995.
Twain, Mark. *Following the Equator: A Journey Around the World*. Minneapolis: American, 1898.
Warren, Max. *I Believe in the Great Commission*. Grand Rapids: Eerdmans, 1976.
Wolters, Albert M. *Creation Regained: Biblical Basics for a Reformational Worldview*. Grand Rapids: Eerdmans, 1985.
Wright, N. T. *The Epistles of Paul to the Colossians and to Philemon*. Grand Rapids: Eerdmans, 1986.
———. "God's Way of Acting." https://www.religion-online.org/article/gods-way-of-acting.
Yancey, Philip. *Disappointment with God: Three Questions No One Asks Aloud*. Grand Rapids: Zondervan, 1997.

www.ingramcontent.com/pod-product-compliance
Lightning Source LLC
Chambersburg PA
CBHW052340230426
43664CB00041B/2504